YOUNG WRITERS

WOT NOT

KENT

First published in Great Britain in 1994 by
POETRY NOW
1-2 Wainman Road, Woodston,
Peterborough, PE2 7BU

CONTENTS

THE LONESOME RIDER

A beautiful lady all elegant and fair,
Was captured by a man who didn't care.
She struggled, screamed but could not flee,
He was too strong and did not let her be.

She was tied, hit and put to the ground,
She was thrown in the water and nearly drowned.
He finally stopped and went away
And did not feed her for a day.

But all of a sudden there came a rider,
A handsome, strong and valiant rider.
He cut his way throughout the thorns
And rode so swiftly through the corn.

He was met so quickly by the man
And hit so hard he could not stand.
He fell to the ground in a pool of blood
And it seemed that he had gone far enough.

She turned around and fell on the bed,
She really thought that he was dead.
But then she heard a voice cry out,
She turned around and was in doubt.

She saw the rider on his feet,
He had cut the man's head off, oh so neat.
He staggered up and opened the door,
To see her tied up upon the floor.

He untied the rope and let her go,
She wanted to thank him but he said no.
He then had mounted on his horse
And resumed the earlier, muddy course.

Danny Jury (14) Borden Grammar School

CLOCK

I have a face and two hands;
Workings of the mechanical mind are my think thing.
I am almost dictatorial in my influence among the masses
For those rigid regimes I maintain.
And time ticks forward as I watch from my vantage point
Upon this familiar wall.

A woman sits, in a chair by the fire.
Every morning she visits my comrade the mirror -
I measure the measurements
Whilst she reflects their effects.
The woman looks up to me and calculates the remainder of the day
And I love her so; or at least would want to
For she is my product, my own sad victim
Though I turn against her day after day
With my own little bombs that tick, tick, tock away.

The sun rises, the night falls.
Days and words orbit around, descending,
Being spent, ascending again.
The woman eats my minutes, but spits out the hours
And casts me looks of love and hate.

Like a prisoner I wear my numbers for identification.
Seconds effervesce from me like deadly gases.
And what I fear is not unemployment,
Or the pains of loss, or dissatisfaction
But the woman down there is such a stranger
Though I see her everyday . . .
I strip the layers away.

Duncan Chappell (17) Dane Court Grammar School

AN ENSNARED EXISTENCE

Reluctantly, dawn lifts the mists from
the shiny, cobbled streets, cursing, as the sun's rays
project gaunt, grey shadows
through the haze of narrow alleys
in which live robbers and rogues.

Daylight forces hungry thieves back into hiding,
misery shrinks into the unknown shadows,
but death carries on, undaunted.

Sun's warmth wakes many,
but some lay still,
these are the ones who belong to the night -
cold body, no life, death.

Night trains sleep,
no noise passes.
Silently the wind whispers leaves
down into the gutter,
rustling, caressing harsh ground.

There is no easy way out of this barbarous life
we relentlessly lead,
our search for warmth and hunger carries on -
indefatigably.

Fast-flying, ever-flowing night races on
in a chariot of darkness,
once again, oppressing the streets.

Vision becomes obscure as mists fall,
the faint smell of gas fills the night,
coughs from the ill cling to the still air
as all gather around the chimney, warmth at last.

Perpetual questions lie, unanswered.
Endlessly taunted by this burden we call - life.

Rachel Anderson (14) Fort Pitt Grammar School For Girls

WHAT IF . . .?

What if . . . you were a fox,
being chased by drooling-mouthed hounds
with razor-sharp teeth and powerful jaws?

What if . . . you were a bear,
taken from your family when only a baby?
Taught to dance,
with chains through your nose
and a ruined face with tears in your eyes.

What if . . . your home was a zoo?
The only surroundings you knew
were made from barbed wire,
being stared at, teased and mimicked by children.

What if . . . you were only there
for others' amusement and pleasure?

What if . . . you were a pet?
No freedom, privacy, a life like hell,
no choices, no decisions, no freewill.

No say in the matter,
not much life to lead.

Animals are what we need.

We have more power,
and their life will turn sour,
if we continue to live like we are.

Rebecca Lone (13) Fort Pitt Grammar School For Girls

FEAR OF THE RIDER

There, capping the hilltop
He stands tall
Glimmering in the dulling light
As the sun disappears behind that hill.

On his back sat a fair maiden
Her long, flowing, golden hair
Fluttering in the breeze
Like curtains at an open window.

Draped across her body
Lay folds of silk
Of the purest white
Shaping round her figure.

Large, watery, chocolate-brown eyes
Looked back at him
Soft and friendly
Yet wary of his presence.

He called out to her
A little scared
He did not want to frighten her
He just said he meant no harm.

She cried out a little whimper
And tugged at the reins
The horse seemed to take off
And fly away over the hills.

Like a silhouette
Of severe black and white
The lady and her great horse
Disappeared and were never seen again.

Ben Travers (15) Borden Grammar School

GLAMOROUS MAGIC

Baton rod, spriggy stick,
Catch those ratties in my flow,
Rot those ratties,
Cook them wild,
And let me gobble,
With bliss delight.

Dusky, murky, shadowy eye,
Let me see that bulky fly,
Off with its head!
And let it dwindle . . . dwindle-splash
dwindle-splat
dwindle-gone!

Slimy, soggy, dripping dewy,
Goblin, soil your flawless noodle!
Make it corrupt,
Scuzzy and nasty,
Then be off,
To do your duty.

Wizardry, sorcery, magical power,
Make reprisal,
For that grotty mortal,
Bewitch him with the devil's power,
To teach that grime,
The moral value.

Glamorous magic,
From the living world,
So let this be the tip of spells,
For it could be too late,
To escape . . . *the shedding tears.*

Jasdeep Channa (14) Gravesend Girls' Grammar School

ST PAUL'S

The church
Stood tall and firm.
Its dark, unlit windows watched,
Waiting,
Apprehensive.

Inside,
Perpetual silence,
Filling every nook,
Every cranny.
The lingering smell of death,
Of mourning,
Enveloped every soul, every being.

All was calm and tranquil,
Except for the wind,
That howled,
And groaned,
Beating on the church door,
'Let me in, let me in.'

The organ played,
Softly,
Sombre,
Foreboding.
The sinister tune
Echoing through every fragment of the church.

And there the boy sat, alone.
His tiny, terrified eyes,
Moist with tears.
He cried and sobbed, but no-one answered,
Nobody heard him.
No-one was there!

Ami Cooper (13) Gravesend Girls' Grammar School

THE WANDERING STAR

The friendless star is fabulous,
An inexplicable spark,
It weaves torched lights across the sky and cuts through solid dark.
A firework that is soundless,
With no crude paper lit,
Too high to handle,
Too fast to capture it.
With no-one to talk to, its problems were not shared,
So when it faded and disappeared,
No-one really cared.
I watched it pass one summer's night,
A fast-moving, streaking light,
How many worlds it must have seen,
With mountains, seas, and evergreen.
When its beauty passes, some people barely blink,
About the lonely shooting-star, people rarely think.
It has simply no-one on whom it could depend,
It has no mother or father,
No family or best friend.
I wonder where it came from?
And where it was born?
I wonder where it goes to when the evening turns to dawn?
I hope, to heaven is where it will ascend,
To find another lonely star,
Of which it can befriend.

Michelle Watts (13) Gravesend Girls' Grammar School

MR DEATH

I feel him, stalking me, in the dark; I panic.
What are the rules?
He can't get you in the light, nor covered up . . . so I
Dive under the sheet, cover myself from head to toe, stop breathing.
Is he there, waiting, by the door, for me to come out, to my . . .
death?
Shall I stay in the bed or shall I *jump!*
Surprise him, run away?
No, that doesn't work. The rules don't apply here.
But I am older than I was, and have more strength than I did!
But does he have more strength than me?
Should I take a chance and risk it?
I tremble, it's decision time.
Apprehensively pull down the sheet, the tiniest fraction, and open my
eyes.
Ahhh! Scream! He is there.
Pull up the cover, phew!
I reach out to turn out the light.
I flick the switch. Light . . .
Where is the light?
The bulb has gone, he took it, I know he did.
He creates his own darkness.
He creates death.
Yours, mine, everyone's.
I cheated him once but he has come back for me.
But there is a chance, the tiniest chance . . . shall I?
'Come join us, it is fun, you will enjoy it,' he whispers hoarsely.
Come on, slip into my sack and die!'
'No!'
Then suddenly, light and he is gone.
Slips through the shadows to claim his next victim.
But he will be back, because Mr Death *never* gives up.

Joanna Burton (13) Gravesend Girls' Grammar School

THE VAIN AND NOSY PEACOCK

The peacock had a big nose,
This made her nosy,
The peacock thought herself pretty,
Although she only had cheeks which were rosy.

As the peacock thought herself pretty,
This made her extremely vain,
As she wasn't at all pretty,
It was decided she had no brain.

She was looking at herself,
And never saw the fox,
Who put her in a trap,
Carting her off in a cardboard box.

When the peacock started wailing,
He told her to behave,
Then it started hailing,
So he rushed her inside his cave.

When she got out of the box,
(Which was now totally soggy),
She asked him why he did it,
He replied, 'It's my hobby!'

She asked lots of questions,
Because she was so nosy,
He fell in love with her,
Including her cheeks so rosy.

Right after they both got married off,
Poor peacock died of a terrible cough,
And the fox went back to bachelor life,
And never gave a thought to his peacock wife.

Rajinder Randhawa (13) Gravesend Girls' Grammar School

SPRING

In the garden,
in the spring.
Daffodils are
opening.

Lambs are jumping,
in the field.
In the distance,
the church bells peal.

Flowers waving in
the breeze.
People recovering from
the winter freeze.

Blackbird sits at the
top of the tree.
Chirping his song,
merrily.

Nights are short,
days are longer.
The light of day,
is growing stronger.

The leaves on the trees,
look fresh and green.
Spring is such a
lovely scene.

Elizabeth Woodward (12) Gravesend Girls' Grammar School

LOVE DIES

'Love dies,' I hear him say;
'You despised her more every day.
You dragged her behind you through the dirt.
You never knew she was deeply hurt.'

I woke up with a cry.
My forehead damp, my mouth dry.
But still that nagging voice would go;
'You've ruined her life, I told you so!'

Beating the pillow with a clenched fist,
Can't see properly, a gloomy mist.
My brother stirring, a muffled groan,
But turns over, back to sleep, with a sigh and a moan.

That voice continues to nag on and on:
'Her spirit is dying, her life is gone.
You evil agent of the dark!
You left a despicable permanent mark.

You lead her on and made her blind
To your injustices so she would never find
Someone who loves her with deepest respect,
In whom a building of hope could erect.'

The next thing I knew, the lights were on,
Family gathered, *the voice has gone!*
That gloomy mist, not in sight.
Never again will I forget that night.

Rebecca Abraham (13) Gravesend Girls' Grammar School

THE DAY OF GLORY

I remembered the posters, the songs they would sing,
Those encouraging words of song.
I remembered the glory they said war would bring,
As the battle slowly raged on.

I tried to think, through the shout to advance,
As the enemy ran for cover,
But now it seems I am given my chance,
For the battle is all over.

I look at the field of numberless dead,
And think to myself, 'How?'
Tales of grandeur filled my head,
But where's the glory now?

I must be a hero now, I guess,
As our side won the day.
Most of my friends lie dead in this mess,
So there's nothing left to say.

The people of London hearing of this,
Will give themselves three cheers,
Saying, 'Wish I was there!' and airing their views,
And they will shed no tears.

They cannot know what is happening here,
Of all the sorrow and strife.
They cannot know this incessant fear
That I live but to lose my life.

These are my thoughts as I look at this place,
Where ten thousand, it seems, have died.
This is the truth which I cannot face,
So behind the glory I'll hide.

Jennie Pocock (16) Highsted Grammar School

YOUR KING AND COUNTRY NEEDS YOU

Fight for your country
How noble, how brave
Be blown up for your country
Does not sound quite so great.

The day has come
For me to run for my country
To run to my death
How stupid I have been.

I am starving
Have not eaten properly in days
They offer me food
No need I say, *I will be gone in a mo.*

I sit hunched over in the trench
My feet frozen to the bone
It is so bitterly cold
Just waiting to die on my own.

All the restless nights I have suffered
From the bombs over head
This is all so pointless
So! It will be over for me in a mo.

The call comes for me to go over
I say goodbye to friends
Gun in my hand I jump
I jump thoughtlessly towards my death.

Amy Church (14) Invicta Grammar School

THE STORM

Sitting straight backed in the car
I watched out the window,
This storm blinding me with its ferocity
Slowly moving forward,
Desperate to get out.

I thought with envy as the tape sang,
I was far from here,
Laughing, dancing with them,
I was wondering quickly,
Far from this terrifying rain.

I was gliding over many lands,
Till I was there.
Outside the light grey guiding,
I ran straight in,
Seeing my goal.

They were practising,
And I knew what to do,
Jumping in, I started,
Laughing, enjoying it,
Like I was supposed to.

The lights turned on,
This was it,
Seeing the audience's faces,
I'd succeed I knew,
All eyes were on me as I began.

All was going well,
I just had the lift with my partner,
I ran towards him,
Threw myself, and started falling.

Falling, nothing to help me,
Just falling, falling . . .
My sister's sharp voice broke in,
I sat bolt upright,
Awakening from my sleep,
Back to the terrifying rain.

Sarajane Bell (14) Invicta Grammar School

YOUR KING AND COUNTRY NEEDS YOU

Your king and country needs you, son
To defeat the enemy,
March proud into the battle, lad
Be brave and set your country free.

Your king and country needs you, son
To fight and then maybe die.
Your wife will receive your medals, lad
Was the painted picture of war a lie?

Your king and country needs you, son
To help dig a deep, damp trench,
Then live with rats and roaches, lad
And starve and bear the sickly stench.

Your king and country needs you, son
To kill an innocent man,
You're there to commit a murder, lad
Across the suicidal no-man's land.

Your king and country needs you son,
To lie in a hospital bed,
You may loose a limb or an eye, lad
Most of your friends are already dead.

Your king and country needs you, son
To help win this war and bring peace,
But what is it that you want, lad?
For this terrible war to cease

Nadia Larouci (15) Invicta Grammar School

YOUR KING AND COUNTRY NEEDS YOU

Go! It's your duty lad.
Do it for your good old dad,
You'll be a hero, you'll fight for a cause,
What are you going to do, sitting indoors?
Do it for the country,
Your country that needs you.

Think of your dear mother,
And how she will be proud,
Think of the dreams you once had as a boy,
And now that you're allowed,
Fight for your country,
Your country that needs you.

Yes, I'm going, I'll fight for my country,
I'll be a hero and make my mum and dad proud,
I'm glad that I'm going now I'm allowed,
I'll be a soldier, and return in glory,
I'll be able to tell my children my story.

I'm fighting the war,
I've seen my friends killed,
The dream I once had,
Has not been fulfilled.
My home is a trench, full of water and mud,
I sleep amongst insects and dried human blood.
I want to be at home.
The way it used to be,
I've made up my mind,
That fighting is not for me.

Michelle Doublet (15) Invicta Grammar School

YOUR KING AND COUNTRY NEEDS YOU

Your king and country needs you,
The sergeant said to me.
You'll soon become a man he
said,
Win medals lad, you'll see
But what he didn't tell me was,
I'd never again be free.

Our awful home it was a hole,
All full of mud and lice.
And there we stood for days on end
Like timid, frightened mice.
Our time on earth reduced to just
A roll of Death's great dice.

Over the top and back again,
Over the top once more.
Each time, lose another friend,
As both sides marked the score.
Where had all the heroes gone?
What was it all for?

Someone told me it was done,
The war was at an end.
The gas, the mud, the guns, the
Dead,
Now enemy was friend,
The empty shells of bodies
Could go home and could not mend.

So I will never be set free
Though the fighting is long done.
And I can sit in my own home
As no doubt, do the Hun.
They're enemy no more, I know
And God's peace defeats the gun.

Laura Davey (14) Invicta Grammar School

THE WORLD

Oh look at the trees,
Green as grass,
Blowing in the breeze,
Soon gone alas.

Oh look at the sky
Blue as the sea,
No birds, they've all died,
No more I can see.

Oh look at the fish
Waggling their fins,
Soon on a dish,
They never win.

Oh look at the dwellings
Replacing the woods,
Which greedy men are selling
To make homely goods.

Oh look at the city
Polluted and grim
And look at the pity
Of the people within.

Oh look at the town
Crowds all around,
Look up and down,
What a sound.

Oh look at the world,
Soon it's all gone,
But it's not too late
To get something done.

Alexis Grant (11) Invicta Grammar School

CASTLE OF SECLUSION

Plodding onwards,
Each step seemingly steeper
Than the last,
Like being in a huge labyrinth
Of entwining stairs.
Round and round
In a circular motion,
Spinning like a spiral,
Never ending like eternity.
The moon does not shine above,
There is no light,
But for the cracked walls.
The only sound is
The echo of footsteps,
All thudding in unison,
The top gets closer
As the ground gets further away.
The final step leaps forward
To catch you unawares,
Slowly onwards
Long and dark it lies,
A passage of ancient memories
And stories untold,
A door lies yonder
But is never reached,
It is too distant,
And yet your hand may reach out
To touch the splintered wood,
Where insects live
In a shroud of rot.

Zoe Forrest (16) Invicta Grammar School

YOUR KING AND COUNTRY NEEDS YOU!

I hear the talk around the streets,
I see the posters on the walls,
But what is all the war about?
Is it just a game for fools?

I see the queues to join the war,
They say my country needs a hand,
Think of all the fame and glory,
Gained from fighting for this land.

Go now young lad, be brave and bold,
Measure up for your uniform,
In years to come we will be proud,
Your family won't have to mourn.

So I joined to fight for her,
And went through times of blood and gore,
But is my simple name remembered?
And has my country gained much more?

In a trench I sat for months,
Without a single glimpse of light,
Every day I grew much weaker,
Barely able to get up and fight.

The brave stepped into no man's land,
Never to be seen again,
The nights grew longer by the hour,
Soldiers were no longer sane.

But still my country needed me,
That's why I lie in this here mound,
Under the stars with many others,
Where the air makes so few sounds.

Jenna Masters (14) Invicta Grammar School

WHAT BROKE THE CHATTER?

Bang, what was happening?
What broke the chatter?
Why were there flames?
I know what's the matter
It was a tremendous bang
That I'm sure we all knew.
The blitz had begun.

We ran for some shelter,
Some left behind.
Then come to my mind,
My family, where were they?
But all I could hear were bangs and loud
Cries.
And all I could think had my family died?

An hour or so later, when silence appeared
We come out of shelter,
All we could see was just what we feared,
Rubble everywhere like a broken helter skelter,
My house was somewhere in there.
Then suddenly
Came to my eyes
Someone I knew
Not in disguise.
I ran and ran as fast as I could
Not caring a bit about the rubble and wood,
The thing that I wanted,
The thing that I knew,
The thing that I'd worried all the night
Through,
My family was safe.

Kate Bowles (13) Invicta Grammar School

UNTITLED

A white dove flies above the clouds
With my heart in it's beak
My emotions soar
My heart pounds
My insides churn
Every time I see you
My tongue is tied
Like a hanky with a knot in it
I try to speak
But only one thing
Comes to mind.
I love you !
Over and over again,
Like a washing machine
Spinning its load
I tell my brain
To do some work
But like a donkey
Being pulled
It does not budge
But still thinks of you.
Fantasy.
I must get better
But at this time
It feels as though I will die!
Love is a poison
There is no cure for!

Siana Sisley (15) Mascall's School

THE BLOOD FEAST

As the light wears out
And the hour hits midnight.
The mass killer reveals his face.
One red eye glowing like a blazing forest fire,
The other slit and blood stained.
This
Sleek
Fast
Skilled
Warrior approaches the blood feast,
Slaughtering a few unfortunate beings on the way.
On arrival he joins with others
And gradually move to a high rock.
Then and only then they howl simultaneously
Once
Twice
And three times.
Then they all dart into a dark forest,
Called the Feast Zone.
Any that stood in their way
Would have a one out of ten chance of surviving,
Suddenly they stop,
They disappear,
Then slowly night gives way to dawn,
Everywhere is filled with light,
The blood feast is over.

Nicholas Janda (11) Ravens Wood School for Boys

A FISH IN THE SEA

Swimming,
Sensing the surroundings,
Relaxing, floating with the tide.
Pink rocks, green plants,
The bottom of a boat, drifting.
Drifting with the tide.
What's that?
Falling, plummeting, over the side of the boat,
Coming, falling, towards me!
Swim, swim as fast as possible!
Safe now, swimming,
Drifting with the tide, relaxing.
Other fish swimming, relaxing.
Drifting with the tide
Bigger, looming,
Looming over me.
Snapping jaws, snapping at me!
Quick, swim, as fast as you can!
Through a small cave entrance,
Too small for the big fish,
Safe now,
Drifting with the tide,
Relaxing,
The worst fear, sharing a plate with chips,
Salt,
Vinegar,
Don't think about that now,
Relax, drift,
Drift with the tide.

Alan P Smith (12) Ravens Wood School for Boys

THE GHOST OF CLASSROOM THREE

There's a tapping at the window,
A moaning at the door
And something ectoplasmic,
Sticking to the floor . . .

Some say it was a teacher
That met a nasty end . . .
She had a class of awful kids
Who drove her round the bend.

Some say it's impossible
And that it's just a story . . .
But classroom three you must admit
Feels different . . . sort of eerie.

She doesn't come out too often,
Maybe once or twice a year,
She wanders around and mutters
Then . . . poof, she disappears.

There's a rapping on the desk tops
There's a rattling at the door
And something trying to get out
Of teacher's locked desk drawer.

But don't panic, don't be frightened,
Don't scare too easily,
It's really nothing special,
Just the ghost of classroom three . . .

Katherine Angell (12) St Edmunds School

WHO CARES?

Nobody cares what's happening,
They just sit and watch it all go by,
They read the paper, full of yesterday's news,
Turning the page, giving a sigh.

But if they just take a look out of the window,
Or look down, birds-eye view,
They'll see the world and what a cruel world it is,
But it will be too late, nothing they can do.

They saw a poor girl on the corner,
As they passed, this time, last year,
Like everyone else they chose to ignore her
And no longer she is here.

Nobody cares what's happening,
They just sit and watch it all go by,
Watch the news, news about the hungry,
Flicking the channel, giving a sigh.

They don't think about the poor and hungry,
They haven't time, far too busy to care,
They're all tied up in their own little worlds,
What's the difference to them if the hungry weren't there?

Then one day they reach into their purse,
Where money they find none.
Like the girl, now homeless and hungry,
Like them, who cares? No-one.

Donna Frith (13) Invicta Grammar School

THE BABY-SITTER

She'll come and sit in our chair,
She'll come and drink our tea,
She'll come and read our paper,
She'll come and watch our TV.

What's in it for us?
It's our chair,
It's our tea,
It's our paper,
It's our TV.

She'll say it's our bedtime,
At quarter past eight!
I haven't done my homework,
Thanks a lot mate!

She'll say go to bed,
All she'll do is nag,
I know I'm not going to like her,
The old bag.

There's a knock on the door,
It's bound to be the witch,
But it's a man,
Someone might have said!

He looks dead fun,
He looks dead cool,
He looks like the baby-sitter,
I look like a fool!

He is dead fun,
He is dead cool,
He is the baby-sitter,
I am a fool!

Anthony Scott (12) The Westlands School

SEVEN AGES OF A TEDDY BEAR

Age one is brand new and shining
Sitting in a warehouse box
Ready to get to the shop
With a rabbit, a frog and a fox.

Age two is on the shop shelf
Watching adults, children and babies,
Will they buy me may I ask?
The answer I think is maybe.

Age three is being played with,
Loved and cared for too.
I am so very happy
Now I belong to you.

Age four is lying on the bed
In a messy tangle of toys
Most of them are awful
Especially the big frog boys!

Age five I've been left in a puddle
Out in a shower of rain
I'm getting old and torn
My stomach's full of pain.

Age six is tattered and torn,
One ear, one eye and no nose,
I thought I would be cared for,
Well, that's what I supposed.

Age seven is lying in the box
Stuck up in the loft
With sad eyes that cannot see
Feeling damp and soft.

Helen Phillips (12) The Westlands School

MY LOVE

I sit by her now, tasting the radiance
Surrendering my love feels like an aeon ago.
I needed her, that was all I knew.
Suppressing her figidity.
And now she's here beside me
My toiled emotions know not what to do.

A once dormant light rules my mind,
The romance that froze, thaws
Freeing love once gripped by hidden clutches.
The scars of the distant past split
Revealing a hot molten mass engulfing,
A woman whom I treasure more than the earth.

Grass glistens with jewel-like droplets
A couple fused together with scary energy,
Crouched, oblivious of their surroundings,
Birds sing with each other in harmony,
Knowledge of the personal miracle
That eliminated the two's floundering.

Atmosphere is pleasantly stifling
Perfume and murmured endearments,
The hair, soft cascading silk,
Sweet kisses with feverish breath
To create nothing before experienced.
There's never any doubt that love's a disease.

Barrie Hickmott (16) The Westlands School

TIME TO GO

As the whistles blew, short and sharp
And tired men ascended the rickety ladders,
I realised this was it.
It was time to go over the top for the first and last time.
The ladder groaned and bowed under our weight.

There was a sudden commotion behind us,
I turned to see a young man being dragged through the thick mud,
His arms and legs thrashing around,
Like he was in some awful nightmare.
He was pleading not to be made to go over the top to his death.

He had been the bravest man I had ever known,
But the waiting had made us all a little crazy.
I turned away and carried on up the ladder,
His frightened face haunted my mind.

As I peered over the trench,
I heard a shower of bullets, screams and finally a dull thud.
I sank down but someone pushed me,
And I was hurled up into no man's land.

It was surprisingly peaceful up there in the dark
As I walked slowly across,
But then,
Whoosh! A flare went up
And we were lit up like Christmas trees.
It wasn't peaceful anymore.

I could feel the bullets cutting my flesh,
But I just stood there,
Mesmerised by the sight of the falling bodies,
Like skittles being blown over by the wind.
It began to grow dark and the world began to sway,
I could feel the cold icy finger of death on my neck as I fell into
Oblivion.

Katherine Jefferiss (15) The Westlands School

REGRET

Haunting my mind,
the shadows of the past,
behind closed doors.
The wrong once achieved can never be erased,
no matter.
The right gained in future times,
and happy once again,
only to fall into a deep sorry pit,
by one unmeaning word mentioned by an ignorant
friend.
It can never be repaired,
hostile,
always looming.
Waiting to seep out at a moments notice,
hoping, praying to recover,
from this unbelievable despair,
I sit alone.
Insane tears roll silently down my blazing
cheeks.
Hoping for the light shining at the tunnels end,
calling me.
I wrench myself out of this sorry state,
closing the doors once again,
but this time the pressure forcing them,
it's not so strong,
but still there.
Waiting impatiently to show itself again,
inspired by the light I decide,
there comes a time to be free of your past.

Heidi Salt (16) The Westlands School

THE DAY OF THE WHALE

In the murky darkness of the night sea,
A child is born,
Not a human child, a whale.
As it brushes past its mother,
The water is electrified with love and affection.
The sand sparkles gold and silver,
From the reflection of the moon on the silent beach.

Whale cries are heard from all around,
Breaking the silence.

Whale hunters!
The word is spread across the sea, danger!
Nothing ventures to the surface,
A harpoon is fired,
The sea turns cold with blood.

Another harpoon is fired,
Skimming the surface of the bloody sea,
A dying battle is fought,
Mother against machine protecting her newborn.

The sea is sorrowful from the disruption on its surface,
The cruelty of humans strikes again,
The piercing speed of the harpoon breaks the mother's skin,
All is quiet again.
A once happy calf turns to face emptiness,
Knowing it will live without love,
And heads into the school of whales, alone,
In which it was born.

Stacey Last (15) The Westlands School

WAR

We've all heard the orders,
We go over the top tomorrow,
It's our turn to die now,
Like all the others before us.

We may as well be dead,
With rats chewing at our faces,
Cause either we go over and Germans shoot us,
Or we're shot in the back for cowardice.

Back to the holes that we live in,
Noise like thunder, hardly ever stopping.
Dead bodies like a carpet,
Made softer by the rats that eat them.

What's going to happen to my family,
Left alone, no money, no hope,
My kids will live with no father,
To have fun with them, or to discipline them.

I've no chance of survival,
Unless I get out of here in time.
But the only way to do that is wound myself,
Because the Germans shoot to kill, not just injure.

I haven't slept for days, partly because of the noise,
Partly because of the rats, who would eat you alive given half a chance,
But mainly due to the pain in my feet, trench foot they call it,
But I don't care what it's called, I just wish I didn't have it.

Morning already, the last dawn I'll see,
But I won't die a coward, I'll go over the top,
I won't make my children think how could he do this to us?
And make them full of shame.

Time to line up and prepare to go over,
I can't see who allows them to do this,
We never get anywhere anyway. The only thing we gain is
more dead in the trenches.
Killed by German and British men.

There goes the whistle, it's time to go,
All I hope is that I die quickly,
And painlessly, or as much as possible,
When shot by the enemy at war.

Samantha Walker (13) Weald of Kent Grammar School For Girls

A CRY FROM THE BATTLEFIELD

Go and make us proud lad, fight for your country; the war will
Be over before Christmas.

God, how wrong he was,
Eighteen months I have been marooned on this cursed battlefield,
Surrounded by death and disease, if only he knew!
My companions who became my friends are now lost to me,
Maybe they are the lucky ones.

Pools of blood cover my feet, flowing like water from a tap,
Bones litter the ground like the soil I once saw before me,
My hands are brittle,
My feet are blood shod,
My heart pounds for my country, when will it end?

I awake despondent,
I know not whether dawn has risen,
All I see are bleak clouds of despair,
My eyes long for the sun as if blinded by darkness,
My body cries out for life when all around me is death,
And my heart yearns for solace as if it were it's very life's blood.

Holly Fairweather (14) Weald of Kent Grammar School For Girls

DEATHLY CONFLICT

The mental torture
The physical pain
The British society proud to watch their men's lives rot away,
Their flesh to decay, bones to become brittle and snap, snap, snap
As easily as the wishbone of the last chicken consumed before this
Bloody tyrant of a war started,
When we were deprived of such foods which we only remember as a
Distant dream and a hope for the near future.
The society, our families not knowing the truth of what really lies
Behind the glorious name of war.

Every soldier is dead, but their bodies still fight on.
No-one any longer has feelings,
They are just limp, uncared for bodies powered by the adrenaline
That they see their loved ones once more
Before the coffin lid is closed upon them.
No man's land, exactly what it says, no men.
You refuse to leave the trenches and you are no man, but coward.
You face the fact that at nineteen years you must brave to enter
No man's land, and don't live to become a man.

War is the name of a two faced scoundrel.
Glory, the side of the uninformed public,
And then the real life tragedy, involving thousands of men,
The blood, the bones, the wasted lives the madness attacking men
From every angle.
The hope for peace and the daunting fear of another war, another
Generation wiped out.
And what for?
Self satisfaction for dictators and leaders.
No consideration for the young men dying, the widowed women crying.

This bloody war, like no other war before.

Alice Cheverton (13) Weald of Kent Grammar School for Girls

A MEMORY OF WAR

Silently, rippling like water
Faintly, like a baby sighing
I hear this war
Like mist driven by the sea
It descends sick and vile
Its stench surrounds and engulfs me
Choking and squeezing every last drop of breath
The sounds are clearer now
I hear the fire of artillery
And the monotonous thud of foot on mud
Men are marching to war
The air is thick with blood
And men's futile screams rent the air apart
Blinding light fill my brain
And shadows of soldiers
Dance like madmen before my eyes
A melody of widows tears
And dirty starving children that
Huddle in small groups and grieve
And then the images fade
And I am on my own
Staring at these lush green fields
Birds fly overhead and the air is sweet and fresh
But beneath me the earth holds its memories
Silent and brooding she locks away those horrors
She knows it will happen again
She knows and she waits.

Sarah Stubbs (13) Weald of Kent Grammar School for Girls

WHO'S RESPONSIBLE?

Is this what I wanted? Was I eager for death?
Bullets flying, striking men at random to their fate,
Why fight for such a bloody war?
Many will die,
Many are dying,
Many are dead,
They tell you it's for your king and country,
What lies, such a pitiful excuse!
I implore you, take a look!
Take a look and what will you see?
A man poisoned by Mustard gas,
A human fountain of froth and blood,
Orange blisters, sore eyes,
Every breath a driven dagger,
Screams of pain, a wail of death,
Held down by ropes to his bed,
Another, a half man,
Lost limbs, hideous heads,
Mutilated men,
Only the lucky ones die,
My death like many others is imminent,
We're not driven to destruction,
It's not death we fear,
We embrace it,
A one way ticket to everlasting freedom,
Over the sorrowful screams of piteous pains,
I hear the words of a man,
Driven out by his final dying breath,
Who's responsible?
I knew his answer,
For in the Army,
Life is not long at all!

Sarah Chamberlain (14) Weald of Kent Grammar School for Girls

SCHIZOPHRENIA

Waking up - all alone,
Lying there - on your own,
Peeping through a window bare,
Without realising you are there.
Your life retreats to the depths of your mind,
Reality's life was left far behind.
You sit there staring, irrational life,
You sit there intent on your own strife.
Your hand shakes, you spill your drink,
Not a sound you utter,
You slowly drift away from there,
Not a word you mutter.
You drift away with all your might,
Your lonesome soul,
Your lonesome flight.
Your thoughts have faded, gone, no more.
Your life is missing, what's left is poor.
They try to love,
They fail to show it,
You try to respond,
They fail to know it.
They observe your hunched figure rocking to and fro,
They observe the doctors have tried all the cures they know.
You know no more, except your thoughts,
Your stress caused this,
You're overwrought
You've escaped inside, and now you're here,
You won't come back, they fear.

Abigail Flynn (12) Weald of Kent Grammar School for Girls

INDIAN LAND

The natural wilderness,
Moulded by God's hand,
The scorched plain for all to see,
This dusty barren land.

This sacred land was once protected,
By the eyes so high,
The ancestors of years past,
The spirit in the sky.

The spirit world of the dead,
Borders near these lands,
The rocks conceal the children,
The cacti leaves mask the hands.

Above the canyons the king does fly,
Magnificent and regal.
The superior crown that reigns the sky,
Of the great Golden Eagle.

The Indian Brase stands alone,
Looking down in thought,
The questions he wondered,
The answers he sought.

The Creator of whiteman,
Their powers of greed,
Destroys this wild territory
More money is their need.

For white comes in the night,
Many and strong,
Breaking our culture and life,
Is this right or wrong?

Kelly Charman (15) Weald of Kent Grammar School for Girls

FIRE

A single careless spark,
A tiny spot of colour,
A twig catches, next a log,
The flames creep higher,
The gentle murmur increases,
Soon it's a roar.
The warming glow spreads further,
Forever reaching, like never satisfied fingers,
Always clutching at the next thing,
Discontent, angry when he is denied,
Soon he is screaming with rage and uncontrollable fury,
Swallowing possessions and chasing lives,
Always victorious,
Another whoosh,
Another ornament is lost,
Another sacrifice to the God whose name is fire,
Many hands grabbing wildly at anything within reach.
Probing for his next victim,
Panic and confusion spread before the oncoming flames,
Humans and animals united with common intent -
To escape the grasp of the predator.
Homes are reduced to nothing more than a pile of ashes,
But still he tears relentlessly on,
Until he can go no further.

With a last defiant flicker, the fire dies,
Leaving only a small black patch and a trickle of smoke,
A reminder of what has been but is no more,
The fallen kingdom of the once most powerful ruler on earth.

Rebecca Hill (14) Weald of Kent Grammar School for Girls

THE SLEEPY FELINE

The sleepy tabby lies down elegantly,
Stretches her legs out across the floor.
She's getting ready for her nap,
Which begins with the licking of a paw.
When her wash is completed,
With velvet fur, smooth as can be.
She curls up in a snug ball,
Sleek and groomed for all to see.
She gives a huge, wide yawn,
And gazes into the skies.
She rests her head in her paws,
And closes those weary eyes.
Dreaming of a delicious mouse or two,
She's soon lost in a heavy doze.
She is so still and silent,
Except for the odd twitching of her toes,
With a beautifully patterned tail,
Which is wrapped around her tight.
The distinctive markings on her back,
Stand out in the evening light.
Several hours later,
The feline arouses very slowly indeed.
Give her a moment to wake up properly,
Then she'll be off for a feed.
But can she be bothered to get up,
She knows only Whiskas will be there,
She'll just have another little kip,
No-one will really care.

Debbie Semple (13) Weald of Kent Grammar School for Girls

THE ADVENTURES OF THE BLOB OF INK!

The blob of ink flew from the pen
as if a bird in flight.
It landed on a piece of bread
before a massive bite.
It landed on the giant slabs of
mouldy bread and cheese.
But as the boy spat it out,
the blob flew out with ease.
It landed on a table and
(eventually) a chair,
It came past here, stayed
a while, then splattered over there.
It landed on the cold black floor
and stopped to catch its breath.
But up above a shoe came down,
had blob met its death?

Lo and behold the person
tripped and missed the blob by feet,
then a bird flew in the door and
landed on a seat.
The bird pecked blob, who shouted
Ow in his tiny voice.
So the bird stopped in surprise,
the blob jumped in rejoice.

All these stories in one room,
makes you stop and think
and these are the adventures
of the tiny blob of ink!

Theresa Stead (12) Weald of Kent Grammar School for Girls

THE HILL

The hill,
The madness, death surely waits.
To take control, capture the blinded
Vision of the soldiers mind.

No knowledge strikes,
The reason for this madness.
No motive, just orders - let it do,
Just ignore this place, forget
This ghostly dream.

Come on, up the Hill Lads,
Why Sir, why?
Orders Lad.
The crackling shakes, and sneers,
Of sky gliding bombs that drift
Pain stakingly towards us,
Causing distress and fear, like the
Ghostly breath of the Devil's Hell.

The casualties are numbered,
Death had come but now had gone,
The Hill is ours now,
But not for long, *Just orders lad,*
Just orders lad!

We live to fight another day,
Yet again to stalk the hill,
The madness place,
Death surely waits to steal what's ours,
Our souls, our bodies, that served
The country, for what belonged,
To everyone.

Nicholas Alexander (16) The Westlands School

BLIND CHILD IN THE GARDEN

As I walk along the path
I feel the slippery moss beneath me.
I take a turn to the right
And feel the soft grass below.

Suddenly I stop.
With my feet I can feel no more path.
I get onto my knees
And feel the wet ground with my hands.

I feel the cool, icy water of the pond
And hear the ripples made by my hand.
I stand up
And feel my way around the hole in the ground.

I hear the song of a bird,
Very high-pitched,
I wonder what the song means
And what the bird looks like?

Suddenly I feel a sharp pain in my side
And realise I am standing beside a rose bush.
The rose smells fragrant and sweet,
The petals feel smooth and silky.

Then a hand slips into mine.
It is my mother's,
Come to take me back to the house,
Away from the dangers of the garden.

Claire Smith (13) Barton Court Grammar School

ONE MAN'S LAST BREATH

He held the glass in his hands,
Then let the ball of fire roll
Down his throat.
He closed his eyes and started
To move on.
All of them lambs to the
Slaughter.
Now the only thing left was to
Wait for the fireworks to
Begin.
The whistle pierced the
Silence.
He ran not knowing where he
Was going, or why?
But the thought of a bullet in
His back pushed him on.
He would never die a coward.
He kept going, then a sear of
Pain shot through him,
Like a knife in his heart.
He fell to the floor.
Visions of his wife drifted
Like clouds in his mind.
He gasped his last breath
And was gone.

Emily Ford (14) Weald of Kent Grammar School For Girls

WHY HIM?

At first he is normal,
Then slowly, slowly he corrodes,
Like rusting iron,
This disease crawls over
His once healthy body.

Relatives stand round,
Thinking of better times,
They all wish it was them,
Not him,
He did no wrong, why him?

He gets worse and worse,
Weak and immobile,
It's hard for him to breathe,
He can no longer eat,
But they love him still.

As day dawns,
The house feels lifeless,
It stands and weeps,
Call the relatives, it must be done,
Cards of sympathy arrive.

Kirstie Amos (15) Barton Court Grammar School

BOSNIA - WHERE DO THEY GO FROM HERE?

Like a nightmare the fighting never ends
And what of all the food we send?
The faces of the children show their pain
And that through war there is no gain.

See the crying on the television screen,
Vicious fighters heartless, cruel and mean.
Out here the gun is the only law,
Leaving people hungry, starving and poor.

Frustrated UN soldiers can't fire back,
No time for funerals with people dressed in black.
People living in a land of confusion,
The gun - an instrument in a symphony of destruction.

Gavin Wilson (15) Borden Grammar School

HOPE

Pride, pressure,
And we all wanted to be heroes.
No one saw through the lies -
Of money, and women, a place in society,
To the reality behind those lines.
The trenches are cluttered;
Some living, some not.
The pain is so bad, we can no longer feel,
And it's only time, that fear of forever,
Until my life is a memory.
And I won't die peacefully,
Unafraid of the eternity in front.
But slowly and painfully along with countless others.
Knowing I've terminated so many,
Of my kind.
And guilt stricken for my country,
Who killed their own brothers.
Anticipate,
Await,
Believe,
Expect,
Rely,
Trust.
Hope - they say.
But now what's there left to live for?

Daisy Hearn (13) Weald of Kent Grammar School For Girls

AUTUMN

Autumn is a time of high winds blowing,
Of leaves changing colour from red to brown,
Then they drop off the trees onto the ground.
People brush leaves away to clear paths,
But they can't stop them playing havoc with the trains' path.
Birds begin to fly south for winter,
To keep them from the nippy, north, wild wind.

As the nights draw nearer and close on in,
Jack Frost is out causing problems for everyone.
He nips the flowerbuds to stem their growth,
As everyone is seen in their warm, winter coats.
The trees go bare as could be seen,
As they look like a fist reaching up to the sky.
The football season is well and truly on,
As in the mud they look to be this season's champions!

Jonathan Akers (14) Borden Grammar School

THOSE COURAGEOUS MEN

Hurtling down tight canyons
Two hundred feet above the desert floor,
Entering enemy aerospace
As those courageous men go to war.

Still three hundred miles to go
And fear rears up its ugly head,
Passing through the combat zone,
Those courageous men could soon be dead.

Three Tornados, six crew and six bombs,
The enemy won't even see the light of day,
The target appears on the *Hud*
And those courageous men lock onto their prey.

With enemy ground forces disabled
And close air support bearing down,
Air to air missiles closing in
And now two of those courageous men are down.

Now heading back for base,
The wing-commander watches his men hit the floor,
Nothing he can do or ever could,
As those courageous men return from war.

Thomas Matthiae (14) Borden Grammar School

AT THE WATER'S EDGE

The forward-flowing froth,
thrives on the emphatic pulses
of Neptune's rod, driving
towards the sun-soaked shingle
shore.
Purling waves gently shimmer
over fragile pebbles, like a
bold, masculine admirer
embracing his lover.
Protecting, caring, defending,
the cool, tender waves are
like the hands of a gallant
knight, carefully caressing
his fair maiden's soft skin.
The serene tide retreats,
eagerly awaiting its next
pebbled engagement.

Paul Lowe (15) Christchurch High School

ABSOLUTION

Let my wings take flight,
From this desolate plain,
And go forth freely and peacefully,
Into the unknown.

Let my feet touch neutral soil,
As my soul touches compassion,
As I go forth to the place,
Of mutual equality.

Let my breath breathe out,
As I enter my restful dominion,
And go forth with fresh respect,
With understanding and contented air.

Let my eyes bear sleep,
From thunderous shrieks,
As I go forth under a new sky,
To simplicity and serenity.

Let my life be at an end,
As my weary body sleeps,
My soul will go forth, over the top,
To embrace the soul of my enemy asleep.

Danielle Scoging (14) Weald of Kent Grammar School for Girls

IMAGES OF FEAR

Shadows,
Things moving of their own accord.
I lock myself away
But the shadows follow me
Wherever I go
Darkness,
And that's where shadows live.
It seems they're multiplying,
Breeding perhaps.
The depths I'd go to for a bit of light
I have my own shadow,
But even that doesn't possess a light side.
My one appears when it's light,
There's no escaping it.
I would rather be in a lion's den,
Or have a gang of tarantulas sharing my bed.
It may be a queer phobia but the shadow haunts me night and day,
Through light and dark
Wherever I go
It sticks to my heels,
Getting bigger when I turn my back,
Then reshrinking when it comes into my visibility.

Russell Cramphorn (12) Dover Grammar School For Boys

A SUMMER'S DAY

The sun shines brightly in the sky
The sky is usually clear
The clouds are white like cottonwool
The birds all sing in tune.

The sun gets brighter as the day goes on
The clouds are still bright-white
The children come out to play their games
The wind is very light.

The sun turns red, it's getting late
The kids go in for tea
When they return to play more games
There's not much left to see.

The sky turns black
The stars appear
The birds all settle down
The little children go back home
And all go straight to bed.

Alan Booth (15) Borden Grammar School

CHRISTMAS TREES

Picture the trees tall and wide
embraced together side by side,
get out the axe and begin to hack
tie it to the car and take it back,
take it indoors see if it fits
get out the tinsel and the other bits,
hang on the holly and put on the ball
stick the angel on top but watch you don't fall,
now the tree is fully complete
go to bed to get some sleep.

Nicola Back (13) Barton Court Grammar School

THE SEA AT NIGHT

I liked to wander along the beach at night,
All seemed still and the sky shone bright.
I could hear the waves against the shore,
Many times I had walked this way before.

The grey sea and the long, black land,
Everything seemed to blend in with the sand.
The sound of the waves was the only noise,
Apart from a few seagulls whose flight was full of poise.

After a mile of sea-scented beach,
I came to the point I wanted to reach.
Again and again the water seemed to cry to me,
Was the voice in my heart, or was it the voice of the sea?

Tony Raistrick (15) Borden Grammar School

AUTUMN

Summer has now just passed by,
The crisp, brown leaves begin to fall
The birds start their autumn call,
On the ground are where the lifeless leaves lie.

All the flowers start to shed their petals,
It starts to get bitterly cold
So more blankets start getting sold,
More hot drinks get made by the rusty kettles.

The trees seem so bare,
The leaves rustle on the floor
When the wind blows there will be more,
It is as if the trees have nothing to wear.

The temperature changes quickly,
The air sends a chill
So more people fall ill,
Take a look outside and all this you will see.

Sujai Murthy (14) Borden Grammar School

THE SAHARA DESERT

Alone,
The Sahara Desert stands,
Sand dunes everywhere,
No-one's coming.

The Sahara Desert,
Such a big frontier,
People stranded,
Dying from thirst.

Where has the water gone?
Where are the oases?
People being tricked,
By the cunning mirages.

Ben Friend (11) Dover Grammar School For Boys

THE FAIR

The night sky blazes with illuminations of psychedelic
colour which encage the string of pearl-like stars, in a
cobweb of brilliant light.

Screams of pleasure from the crowded rides battle to be
heard above the ferocity of diesel-fed engines as they
plunder the fairground's carefree atmosphere.

Diminished by the rays of entangled light, the
shapes and sizes of the fair's grand attractions,
addict the onlooking mortals with wonder and fear.

As the fragrance of white cotton-candy
drifts through the chilled night air, the noses of children
explode in a frenzy of jubilation at the wild and
fluffy taste of the hairlike gloss.

Chris Payne (15) Christchurch High School

CUP FINAL DAY

Last Saturday was cup final day,
All the lads gathered round to watch Man U play,
Sheffield started well, keeping the ball low,
To help keep Man U up on their toes.

The pitch was great; nice, short, cut grass,
Good for the team who rely on their pass,
The stands were full, ready to burst,
Wednesday fans cheered for Paul Warhurst.

At half-time the score was still nil-nil,
I don't know what the managers' said, but both teams were out for the kill,
Man U wanted a penalty, but nothing was seen,
But it didn't really matter, as the winning goal was scored by Roy Keane.

Lee Johnson (15) Borden Grammar School

SEA BATTLE

The grey coats of
Metal battleships
Built to destroy and kill
Slowly glide their way through
The dark, blue sea.

Two great, grey boats meet
Both enemies of each other
So forthwith a battle begins.

Gunshots and missiles
Fill the air
Until through the smoke
The two great battleships
Slowly sink into the dark, blue sea
Leaving only death and destruction
And a useless existence.

Liam Daniels (14) Borden Grammar School

THE COUNTRYSIDE

The gentle breeze, blowing through the trees,
The buzz of bees and the sound of rustling leaves.
The smell of flowers and the sweet nectar held within,
The foxgloves that tower, above daisies and buttercups and oxlips.

The different grasses, varied in size and shape,
The flowing air, causing some to drape.
The tiny insects, such as caterpillars and grasshoppers,
The small froghoppers, that feed off the sap of plants.

The wild animals, that roam between the trees,
The timid rabbits, that dig holes with ease.
The sly foxes, that carefully hunt their prey,
The cumbersome mole, which has poor sight during the day.

The short-eared owl, magnificent in flight,
The pheasants and kestrels, beautiful when in sight.
The robins and bluetits can be seen in their nests,
With caterpillars and slugs to eat, which to gardeners are pests.

Searching through some countryside,
Ponds and lakes can be found, with many things to hide.
Waterweed and tadpoles and beetles and newts,
Are just some of the creatures lurking in the depths.

Then the rain comes to quench the plants' thirst
And to fill the ponds, sometimes making them burst.
Soon the sun comes out, allowing plants to flourish
And algae to occur, in lakes and ponds.

David Hart (12) Barton Court Grammar School

LONELINESS

It's time for the party, horror movies and a sleepover.
I hate horror movies. I am the only one who is not going.
I wondered all that day what would they be doing?
What would they say about me not going?

I feel lonely, like on the beach when
everyone is playing cricket and I'm not.
Everyone else is going and I'm not,
everyone will be laughing and having fun.
And I will not.

I will tell you about that day of loneliness.
It was like sitting on a bench in a park
when everyone is playing and no-one can see me.

Loneliness is like you could even fly in the sky
and no-one would notice you,
loneliness is like you're in a supermarket
and you knock down a block of tins
and still no-one notices you.

Loneliness is like being all tied up.

That is loneliness.

Emma Quirke (11) Fort Pitt Grammar School For Girls

THE TOAD

Glistening, listening
In the night.
Breathing quietly,
Smooth and fat,
Big, black eyes,
Round and slimy,
Glistening, listening
In the night.

Chris Hodgson (11) Dover Grammar School For Boys

SO BIG, SO BRIGHT

Sparks from around a finitely, small point,
Within is everything,
So compact,
So tight,
Fighting to break out,
Expanding with greed, filling nothing but spite.

Bright lights sparkle in dark, blue clouds,
Circling each other creating new light,
So big,
So bright,
Bringing warmth and pure energy to all that surrounds.

Celestial bodies circle these stars,
From which is a new lease of life,
Life so precious,
Life so pure,
All to be lost by one damn war.

Tim Welsted (15) Borden Grammar School

THE CROCODILE

The crocodile is a fearsome creature
With teeth as sharp as knives,
It is green and brown with lots of lumps,
It is found in rivers and in jungle swamps.

The crocodile is very strong,
It could wrestle with a boat,
It will kill you if you treat it badly,
But mostly leave you alone.

The crocodile has a cleaning bird
Who even cleans its teeth,
The crocodile doesn't chew it up
Because he knows it does him good.

Luke Tridgell (12) Dover Grammar School For Boys

FEAR

'Hello,' my voice echoes of the dark,
My pace quickens again,
'Hello, come out.' The only answer is my own breath.
The dark seems to be closing in around me,
A suffocating, impenetrable cloak, woven by evil and dark.
I stop! There behind me; a noise!
Again I start, my pace quickens to just below a jog,
My imagination starts playing games, visions of horror.
I dare to look left, the woods meet me with a viscous snarl,
Spiky branches reach out, clutching with bony fingers,
Death himself is stalking me, now I can hear his coarse breath,
I can smell the rotting flesh that clings to him,
I can almost feel the bloodlust,
I now hear the army that follow him,
The army of the undead!
They sing chants,
Probing my sanity, they are coming, they are coming . . .

Stuart Dodd (12) Dover Grammar School For Boys

FEAR

The trees loom above,
The night is dark
And the moon casts many shadows,
In each shadow is a hiding killer,
My heart beats faster,
My legs move faster,
The shadows pass quicker,
The shadows grab at me,
I start to run,
The shadows shout,
'Don't go, stay with us, stay.'

David Burkimsher (12) Dover Grammar School For Boys

FEAR

The hammer strikes the anvil of terror,
Blood disappears from my body, immobilising it,
The white monster of fear creeps up,
My brain begins to spin,
Making no sense of anything,
Fear enters the body through anywhere it can find a way in,
The white spider of fear crawls up my back,
Fear begins to take over,
Cackling as I give up calmness,
Taking over my soul,
Fear takes its pleasure,
And slowly dissolves my mind,
Leaving nothing but a body full of terror,
Now fear sneaks away,
Scouring the earth for its next victim.

Steven Perkins (12) Dover Grammar School For Boys

THE OLD MAN

The old man's beard is snow-like,
White as cottonwool,
His eyes are unhappy,
Remembering his wife and family,
The colour of stormclouds,
The colour of lead.

His face is like a creased cloth,
Like a rocky cliff.

His eyes continue to stare,
On and on at nothingness,
Remembering his brother,
His father and mother,
Lonely, all alone.

Mark Callanan (12) Dover Grammar School For Boys

A FISH

Silvery streak in trickling blue,
Eyes are still yet alert,
Scales shine as if they were new.

Jumping jagged rocks clear,
Skimming above sand at speed,
Almost it seems without fear.

Alas, a man stands, submerged to the knees,
A sudden movement and he sees,
A silvery streak and moves in closer,
A squirming salmon for his supper.

Jonathan Hughes (12) Dover Grammar School For Boys

OYSTER, OYSTER

Oyster, oyster
Of the deep
Holding its pearls
Oh so carefully.

On the seabed
Eating till dusk
Better close up
And sink into the sand.

Diver in rubber
He's got a knife
In it goes and twists around
The pain is immense.
Up he takes you
Strips you of your pearl
Rips off your partner
And leaves you to boil.

Richard Darrall (11) Dover Grammar School For Boys

LONELINESS

You feel lonely when you start a new school without your friends,
And you can't wait for the schoolday to end.
But on the way home,
The sky starts to moan.
You wish you were in a nice, warm bed,
And not having to write in cold, grey lead.

You feel lonely when you are ill in bed,
And you have an aching head.
Your mum won't let you watch TV,
But instead just says, 'Get some sleep!'
You know she is right,
But you've tried and tried.
Instead of going out,
You have to stay,
Inside.

You feel lonely when you lose your mum in a shopping centre,
Or when you lose your friends,
But of course you find them in the end.
When you do, they have a go at you,
And you feel lonely again.

Samantha Adley (11) Fort Pitt Grammar School For Girls

THE PURPLE CRYSTAL

A mauve crystal gleaming in the moonlight,
Valuable gift, glistening in the caves.
Sharp spikes from a cliff-face,
Overhanging on a ledge.
Gradually slipping off the stone bank,
Falling, falling, falling down into an endless pit.
Gone, gone forever!

Steven Laycock (11) Dover Grammar School For Boys

THE OYSTER

Down in the darkest shadows of the seas
The oyster spends its time among fish,
Its saucer-like shells, guard and hide its treasured pearl
Away from the merchants of the world,
One day in the darkest shadows of ocean floor
A diver swims down,
Knife in hand, with a torch shining on the seabed
A sudden twisting and turning alerts the oyster,
As human hands go for the precious pearl
A sudden jerk comes to be,
As a knife bursts through the uneven shell
Getting through to the white, clean pearl,
The oyster struggles but it is much too late
The shell shatters and the diver gets away
With the treasured pearl of the world,
Leaving the oyster to die away
In the salty waters of the silent world.

Xavier Taylor (11) Dover Grammar School For Boys

UNTITLED

Could our whole existence be, but just a dream?
For no-one knows, but I, what I have seen.
The sparrows that suddenly sing their song at morn.
The golden beauty of sun-kissed clouds at dawn.
The glistening of stars and the moonlit sky.
When I perceive such sights, I wonder why . . .

Why, with such beauty, is this world an ugly place?
Where innocent people are slaughtered because of their race.
Where starvation exists and slaughtered souls will die.
Where bloodshed, misery and pain, make people cry.
Could this be, the true world that I see
Or are you dreaming, just as much as me?

Carley Carter (16) Gravesend Girls' Grammar School

FROM THE BEGINNING TO THE END

Space.
An empty void of darkness,
An eternal nothingness,
But in it lingers things powerfully beautiful.
Made by a will,
A will unknown,
A will which gave us the most precious thing we own.
Life.
Man takes this gift for granted,
And abuses his sacred home.
His lifeline.
Now man is losing his gift,
Man needs to stop the destruction,
The destruction of himself and his lifeline.
Man knows not what he is doing
And soon, it will be too late.

Caroline Prado-Marin (14) Gravesend Girls' Grammar School

SEA OF COLOURS

The sea,
A clear turquoise that waves to the azure
Sky,
And the pearl-white clouds gather together
On the dark-indigo night.

The early morning amber sun starts to rise
And an ivory fog starts to cover it,
And it starts to rain.

The jade grass starts to cry as it is dribbled
On,
And the chrome fish flee,
As the tide pushes them ashore.

Lisa Harrison (11) Gravesend Girls' Grammar School

THE FOX

His bright, red coat
Blowing in the night breeze,
The trees in the wood
Swaying from side to side.

The fox is sleek
The fox runs swiftly,
His brush is smooth
And he's sweating from running.

He is down in his den
Snug and warm,
He's all alone
With nobody to disturb him.

Sneakily on the farm
Ready to pounce on his prey,
Until snap! And he runs
Away from the danger.

Steven Marsh (11) Dover Grammar School For Boys

FRIENDS OF THE EARTH

I never really could imagine
the earth so dull and grey.

We have got to stop it, now, today.

All the trees are polluted and dying,
not a single bird is flying.

I'd like to see the world as it is,
not the earth in a great, big tizz.

But now I am glad to say,
that I am a Friend of the Earth.

Sarah Freeman (12) Gravesend Girls' Grammar School

PEACE

Peace is a young baby who is not ready to face the world,
Many nations dream of her, although she never comes.
The world is not ready to accept her into their rifts and fears,
For they still do not realise that her brothers are here.
Her family is all that's good,
Peace, hope, charity, gentle children meek.
Freedom, equality, belief; fiery spirits burning men,
Kindness, grace, love, difficult teenagers all over the place.
Gentleness, trust, the parents' guides,
Many feel peace does not care, that she does not ache.
She longs to spread her dove-like arms and hold the world,
She wants to give the greatest gift to mankind,
But still a child, meek and mild,
One day she'll surely come.

Caroline Slater (12) Fort Pitt Grammar School For Girls

CAN YOU HEAR ME?

Can you hear me sir?
Can you hear me ma'am?
I'm alone, totally alone!
You can't hear me now.
I'm away from you.
All of you.
I'll not regret it.
No more troubles now.
No grown-ups to stop my fun!
They never listened then, why should they listen now?
I won't miss them.
Honest.
They won't notice I'm gone.
They won't notice I've run away!
Will they?

Helen Spencer (11) Gravesend Girls' Grammar School

THE TRAVELLER

As the sickening heat falls heavy on his back,
he trudges along, alongside the track.
Shields his eyes from the spherical flame
that seems to choke him with a teasing moisture.
Gazing ahead, the horizon is distant
but he thinks about his past land.
Conforming to images, facing reality,
confronted by himself, rejected morality,
incest and violence
reign his world.

As an innocent child
plagued by images of evil
his mind twisted,
his life marred.
Now he starts afresh
or so they say,
people will help him
or so they say,

But I think he is here to stay.

Kate Waldner (13) Highworth Grammar School for Girls

THE FROG

Eyes popping out,
Staring frantically at me,
Just about to leap,
Strong hindlegs wound up ready,
Fatness of the frog,
Bulging outwards like a fat dumpling,
Lovely shiny finish,
Skin like slime,
Suddenly it's gone!

Oliver Lansley (12) Dover Grammar School For Boys

THE DRAGON

The maiden's gone,
Quick get a knight,
Someone who's bold,
Strong and can fight.

There he goes,
On his trusty steed,
Ready to do,
His heroic deed.

Right, now dragon,
You're for it now,
Give back my maiden
Or casplat and capow!

Just stop for a minute,
It's always the same,
The maiden gets rescued,
The dragon gets slain.

So think of the dragon,
As he's beaten about,
This happens to him,
Week in and week out!

Glen Sansom (14) Mascall's School

UNTITLED

The curly piece of tree
A cobra standing guard
It's back curving round
Into a spiral of intrigue
The shedding of the skin
Like the peeling of the bark.

Darren Hendley (15) Mascall's School

SNOWGOOSE

In the late spring dampness
On the lonely shores of the great marsh
The wilderness ever present
Spread over the half submerged meadowlands
Restless meandering rivers:
Curling round the desolate expanse of reeds
Muffled noise of wildfowl
And the splattering tune
Of seagulls walking on water
Low talking of oyster fishermen
Looking up into the grey cotton skies.

Simon Wilson (13) Mascall's School

LONELINESS

It echoed through the marshlands,
A cry for love and laughter,
The river wept upon the shore,
A cry for life and spirit,
Water blackened with ruptured stones,
Mark the spot where tears have fallen,
Birds circling round a place of rest,
Indication of an ended life.

The sea gallops towards the shore,
Kicks up its rippled blanket,
It whispers softly to the land,
Bring some human habitation
The marshes reflect golden fire
The sky is alight once more
The lighthouse bulb is dying,
Leave me to rest in peace.

Emily Spooner (13) Mascall's School

FIREWORKS

The crackling, the popping, the flames start to
Purge,
As a fiery monster begins to emerge,
The spitting sparks, the roaring flame
Climbing higher and higher, no longer tame.

The fireworks waiting, now to ignite,
Colour the sky for a glorious night.
Exploding, flashing, sparkling blaze,
Reflecting bright in the children's gaze.

The people watching at the sight,
Ohhing and ahhing in devilish delight.
The fireworks gone, the embers glow,
There's more to that monster, more than you
Know.

Lorna Dadson (14) Mascall's School

FRIENDS

They walked off without me again,
They never wanted to be my friend,
Once they found out.

The teacher told them
And they pretended for a while to be my friend,
But I wasn't when they found out.

They thought I was great,
When I told them I was rich,
But now they found out.

It was my fault, I only did it for a joke,
But they found out I was a cheat and liar,
Now I have no friends.

Chloe Washbrook (11) Gravesend Girls' Grammar School

ALONE

A marsh
The sea laps at the roots
Clinging to them
Like a child leaving its mother
For the first time.
Silent but for the few ducks
Laughing like drunken policemen
Their laughs echo for miles around.

A lighthouse
Standing alone on the misty shore
A reject of the world it used to know
It's stripes dark and colour lost
Like a convicts suit
But its heart kind
Like the glow of its light
The wind its one companion
Both glad, but alone.

Joanna Green (14) Mascall's School

IN THE CROWD

Exiting with the crowd,
flowing as a stream,
a bottle neck,
elbows, shouts,
snapping jaws, trying to eat
hungrily closing, opening.

Free flowing,
then, once again,
a bottleneck
and again more doors.

Carla Maxted (15) Mascall's School

HORSES

Smooth and tall like a wall,
Tails like brown, long, lady hair,
Eyes big and dark-brown,
Hooves hard and round.

Ears like blades of coloured grass,
Noses wet like blue raindrops,
Teeth yellowed and white like egg-yolk,
Chestnut like a walnut on the back of a leg.

You mount the brown, shiny saddle,
You walk slowly on like time,
Fast, fast now in trot,
Like a train leaving the station.

You canter up and down like a seesaw,
A wonderful feeling,
You slow down, down, down,
Stop, you slide off like on a slide.

You take off the brown saddle,
You fetch the food, like lightning it begins to eat,
Now at the end, it's time for home,
Goodbye! Goodbye! . . . Goodbye!

Michelle Walters (11) Highworth Grammar School for Girls

UNTITLED

Where is the beginning?
Where's the end?
Time's arrow,
So difficult to bend,
Those broken promises,
What they meant,
Those love letters,
I never sent.

Rachel Bourner (15) Mascall's School

PREDATOR

In the jungle lurks a predator
That feeds on raw red meat
Of an animal slaughtered in its tracks
By the claws that hide in its feet.

Hypnotic eyes of emerald green
Glistening in the light
Docile by day
But menacing by night.

Immense sharp incisors
Surround its gaping jaw
Gripping on a wind pipe
Till its victim breaths no more.

Fur a burnt tanned orange
With stripes of black all round
India is the country
Where these great beasts are found.

Extinction stalks this species
It's man who is to blame
This animal proud and kingly
The tiger is its name.

James Croud (13) Holmesdale Community School

DOLPHIN

Days of fun are
On the run down because
Life is endangered by
People's fishing nets. The dolphin needs
Help from people. Otherwise
In days soon the dolphin will
Never come again.

David Gandon (13) Holmesdale Community School

SAVE THE ELEPHANTS

No longer shall we roam,
For decorations for your home,
We die for ivory
Nothing else!
Or maybe the odd elephant
Skin belt.

A long nose, like a hose;
Long sharp tusks,
Small bloodshot eyes,
Ears like two large fans,
The giant of the animal kingdom,
These big friendly giants,
The innocents of the world.

Carly Howell (12) Holmesdale Community School

GIANT OF THE WOOD

Hunted for its tusks,
Struggling to survive,
Nearly becomes extinct,
Their kind diminishing as we think.

It is a giant big and grey,
Stamping through the forest,
One minute slow and quiet,
Next hooting its trunk!

Watched in fright,
Step by step,
They are all lonely and sad.

The elephant trips,
The net comes down,
The hunter's won,
It's life is done.

Robert Cook (13) Holmesdale Community School

THE WHALE

The whale is a beautiful creature,
So magnificent and strong,
As they glide through open waters,
With their young at side,
They seem so peaceful without a care,
But, do they realise?

Over the horizon come man in their millions,
All after the same thing,
As they move in close,
The whales don't stand much of a chance,
Eventually they are slaughtered
And the great whales are pulled to shore,
Where they are then dismembered
And blubber stripped,
Is all this killing really necessary?

Hannah Goodfield (12) Holmesdale Community School

TIGERS

The hunters set their foot traps,
The tigers roar in vain,
Then a tranquilliser hits it,
It looks in so much pain.

The patterned face, the
Big wide eyes
Glistening in the sun.
How could we kill such a wonderful
beast with the power of a gun.

Lurking in the bushy jungle,
Waiting for their lunch,
The wonderful purring tigers,
Roam around in a massive great big bunch.

Joanne Telling (12) Holmesdale Community School

TURTLES

Deeper, deeper down he'll go,
Down to depths no man will go,
One deep breath is all he needs,
To take him to the place he feeds.

Soon it may not have a shell,
In the shops it soon will sell,
Killed by gun or hook or loop,
Then in a pan to be cooked as soup.

Extinct it will be made by man,
Unless there is a killing ban,
No longer should it be part of a feast,
This innocent, graceful, swimming beast.

Michelle Goodyer (13) Holmesdale Community School

PANDA

I see a panda in its cage,
It's shiny fur black and white,
She's full up of food but empty inside,
She never sees day or night.

She should be roaming free and wild,
Not an exhibit for people to see,
She should be out looking after her young,
It doesn't seem fair to me.

Just a few more years before the panda's extinct,
The last one may have gone,
When the last one's alive are locked away
It seems to me something's gone wrong.

So when she looks at you with tears in her eyes,
Please don't ignore her plea,
She's just saying to you
Help me.

Kate Bartholomew (13) Holmesdale Community School

MY SHY FRIEND

Oh, how I could stand and admire all day,
Those intelligent eyes that seem to say,
I'm afraid my dear, I have no time to play,
Because I am king of all I survey.

I am old and grey and have seen many years,
I have jumped with joy and cried many tears,
But I don't want you to worry, my dear,
Because I am big and strong and have no fear.

My laugh is infectious, my smile is wide,
I pound on my chest with obvious pride,
Don't be afraid, don't run and hide,
Come and talk, be by my side.

I know I am a large and powerful beast,
But fruit and nuts are my sumptuous feast,
One of these days my life will cease,
But until then, all I want is to live in peace.

Suzanne Dack (12) Invicta Grammar School

INSOMNIA

The dark crept into my bedroom,
Silent, as if searching for prey,
Soon my room was solid and black,
'Twas plain to feel, the dark was back.

I could sense it sleeking towards me,
As it wrapped me in its arms,
I was becoming a part of the night,
Oh, if only I could reach the light.

I felt the world slipping away,
As I was swallowed by the shadow,
Will I survive another night?
Only if I win this fight.

Charlotte Norton (14) Invicta Grammar School

ANON

Here lies a solider,
Brave, so they say,
He killed at least twenty,
Day, after day,
The lives that he ended,
The sorrow he caused,
Would never have happened,
If there weren't any wars.
He died doing duty
And it seems such a shame,
That he fought for our country,
Yet we don't know his name.

Sarah Woolven (13) Invicta Grammar School

YOUR KING AND COUNTRY NEEDS YOU

Onwards march, towards the war,
Uniforms smart and freshly washed,
Soldiers bubbling with excitement,
Hoping to gain honour and respect.

Onwards march, towards the war,
The day has come to say goodbye,
Fear and excitement flying high,
As tears and rain fall to the ground.

Onwards march, we're at the war,
Uniforms muddy and smelly too,
Soldiers hopes are crushed,
As they wait in dread of being killed.

Onwards march, we're at the war,
The days last forever and more,
The fear is high and hopes are low,
As they wait for news to go home.

Serena Law (14) Invicta Grammar School

THE CARP ESCAPES

The eager carp angler scurries along the bank like a mouse,
Seeing the potential of the watery expanse in front,
Pitches camp as a Boy Scout would,
No time to waste,
Launches the trap spiced with barbed content,
Beware the carp!
Fooled by the bait like a circus coming to town,
Up like a rocket, the rod becomes part of the horizon,
The carp is an Olympic sprinter striving for the line,
The anger, a heavy weight tries to slow it,
The unthinkable occurs,
All is slack - the carp escapes.

Andrew Kennett (16) Mascall's School

THE KESTREL

I watch the great bird with enormous splendour
Flying gracefully
Peacefully
Through the air
He knows more about life
Than a fish knows the sea
More than the lion knows
The jungle
More than the birds and the bees
Then the gracefulness is broken
By a sharp turn of the head
The peacefulness is shattered
By a sharp high screech
The great bird swoops
And clutches his reward
A defenceless mouse
Gives his life
For a kestrel.

Mark Foley (12) Ravens Wood School for Boys

UNION JACK

Fluttering as the breeze catches the silk,
Standing out miles away,
On a giant metal pole,
The colours of Britain,
Red, white and blue,
Something for Britain to respect,
It's the sign of hope for people in need,
Pride for our winning team.
The sign of the Queen,
Raised in her honour,
Raised with the national anthem,
For people who are triumphant.
You are one among thousands,
Who respect their flag
And are proud . . .
. . . Proud to be British!

Michael Errington (11) St Edmunds School

AN AUTUMN FEELING

The leaves bustle and twirl,
the breeze is cooling.
A golden layer of leaves covers the land
and the sun gleams gallantly.

Light and dark browns fill the air,
the leaves are crushed beneath your footsteps.
Children throw the leaves in happiness
and a tremendous colour is sighted.

All the evenings become dark
and a miserable sorrow falls upon the night.
Everything is silent and deserted
and only the fire crackles and puffs
out black smoke.

Philip Turner (11) St Edmunds School

DEATH TO CAESAR

The Gods are angry
The Gods are mad
Sending prodigies
All things bad
Moving sprinting
Sneaking around
Watch out for the guards
Don't make a sound
Dagger blood tempest gore
The excitement's mounting
Sweating more
Fire spirits near and far
Come on men let's kill Caesar!

Neil Gladwell (13) Northfleet School for Boys

MY LUXURY POOL

It's so lovely just lying by the pool
And having a drink that's nice and cool,
Jumping in when we want to,
There's a big splosh around you.
I'd love to stay here forever,
With just me and my friend Heather.
This is the life for me,
It's where all of you would want to be,
I feel sorry for you people who aren't here,
We're just relaxing and having a beer.
Soon all of us will have to go,
That's the only bad thing about it though,
I'm going to be sad when it is all over,
Driving all the way back to Dover,
Oh well! We'll be back in a year,
You'll be able to hear us all cheer,
I really do love it here!

Anna McDade (11) St Edmunds School

YOUR KING AND COUNTRY NEEDS YOU

Shining new buttons,
Newly made coat,
Everyone excited
And the soldiers gloat.

Streets lined with people
Cheering you on
With a brave expression
Their face it's upon.

Honour and glory
Fill up your head,
Looking at the trenches
You wish you were dead.

The screams of death sound
From far away
But getting closer
Claiming you today.

An early grave stone,
Not enough time.
Forgotten memories,
Buried in grime.

Karis Mulley (15) Invicta Grammar School

CHILDHOOD

Childhood is being too young to do this
Childhood is being too old to do that
Childhood is being too thin or too fat
Childhood is being an angel or brat.

Childhood is doing what seems the most fun
Childhood is eating cream cakes and iced bun's
Childhood is learning what's wrong from what's right
Childhood is knowing when to keep out of sight.

It's Saturday morning the weekend is here
You awake with a smile feeling full of good cheer
There are things that you'll do that will make you feel good
Then you'll get into trouble, *well that's childhood.*

Sometimes it seems that nobody cares
So you sulk in your bedroom or
Just sit on the stairs
Then your mum say's *oh ok well maybe you could*
Help her with the baking, well that's childhood.

Donna Mercer (14) Invicta Grammar School

SPORTS DAY

Ready, steady, go!
And you zoom down the track
as fast as you can,
legs in the air,
flying all about,
till you reach the finish line
and you're all puffed out.

'Wherever you come, first, second, or third in your bout,
it's not the winning, but the taking part that counts.'

But at the end of the day
when the presentations come,
there's no medal for taking part.

Paul Page (11) Dover Grammar School For Boys

THE TURTLE

Tightly packed in that stone-like shell,
Under the pebbles of the beach,
Reluctantly thrashing about, front legs flapping,
Trying to escape that smooth, shiny shell,
Leathery skin like an old horse-saddle,
Elegantly breaks out, like ice on a frosty night.

Gareth Lee (11) Dover Grammar School For Boys

DEMOLITION NOTE

A tune of sadness played,
as the last of the demolition gangs
moved in.

The big iron ball was swung,
onto the remaining empty houses.
The crane seemed to stick on a note
which was repeated in a vibrant
pulse.
The pulse of destruction.
Brightly coloured plastic curlers,
crumpled hats
and fractured pipes
were all that remained, among the
jagged glass and rubble.
Rough laughter filled the air,
as a dislodged chimney pot decided
to fall,
Ricoheting from point to point
on the pile of distorted masonry.

Katherine Thompson (12) Sedgehill School

THE ADDER

The Adder, a most amazing animal
So sly, so quick, so clever.

His forked tongue slipping quickly in and out,
It's a sign of wonder to us but the sign of
Death to its prey.

He opens his mouth hissing madly
His giant fangs gleaming in the sun
His tongue slipping in and out like the devil
Prodding its victim.

He is great at hiding, waiting for its prey ready
Ready to move so quickly and sink its teeth into it.

He has spotted a mouse scuttling across the open
Ground,
He sees his chance and makes a dash, snap too late the
Adder has got him.

Small movement from the Adder as it injects its lethal poisonous
venom into
The mouse, the mouse lays still, motionless one gulp and its gone
down the Adders throat.

The Adder slithers back to its hiding place waiting for its next victim.

Colin Adams (11) Ravens Wood School for Boys

THE LONELY BOOK

This cupboard's cold and dark.
Here I lie untouched by human hands.
People pass me by but do not notice.
I'm out of date, damp and old.
Will I ever escape this prison?

The door opens, a girl hovers,
She picks me up and reads my name,
Puts me down and walks away.
The door shuts and sunlight fails.
Back in the cold and dark I lay.

My luck has ceased.
Nothing to look forward to but dark
And gloom.
Will I ever escape this jungle,
Before I crumble,
Or will I be wiped from
Existence.

Sarah Hamilton (14) Invicta Grammar School

THE LONELY LAND

The Great Marsh -
One of the last wild places of England,
The lonely land.
The low, far reaching expanse of grass and reeds,
The half submerged meadowlands,
The mud flats and tidal pools,
The restless sea.
Desolate,
Only the cries of the wildfowl:
Wildgeese, gulls, teal, widgeon,
Redshanks and curlews.
Human habitants; there are none,
But blackened and ruptured stones -
The abandoned lighthouse.

The lighthouse, housing one human habitant,
A lonely man.
His body warped, but his heart filled with love.

Natasha Speaight (14) Mascall's School

LONELINESS

Lonely,
Lonely in the Great Marsh of Essex,
The last of the wild places of England.
Grass and reeds,
Meadowland that ends at the pool near the restless sea.

It is desolate.
Utterly lonely and made lonelier by the cries of wildlife.
Greys and blues and soft greens are the colours of the
Skies.
Lonely colours.
The waters of the beaches and marshes,
Reflect the cold and sombre scene.

At low waters, the blackened and ruptured stones of the
Lonely lighthouse show above the surface.
Like the top of sagging fence posts.

Inside the abandoned lighthouse is a lonely man.
A man whose heart is filled with love for wild and
Hunted
Animals.
This man has no friends but the wildlife,
He is lonely like the old lighthouse.

Louisa Williams (14) Mascall's School

ONE IN A MILLION

She stands,
Deformed and out-of-shape,
Misplaced and alone,
Pain and agony in her heart,
Like a thousand needles digging,
Her hand reaches out for friendship,
But rejection is all she gets in return.

No care or kindness,
Only cruel and harsh names,
Help! she cries: suffering,
Help! she screams.
No-one hears her pleas,
No-one comes to her rescue.

No pretty faces,
Silky blonde hair,
Big blue eyes,
But:
Inner beauty and strength,
Bravery and courage,
Like a mighty lion,
She's one in a million.

Victoria Tomlin (13) Mascall's School

JOHN PAINE

Twinkling blue eyes and a fervent mind
A grey fuzzy beard covering all of his chin
A man with some memories to tell.

As you drive in your car at sunset or sunrise
He's bound to be standing there watching you pass.

Daffodils will always remind us of him
Flowers that dance in the sun
They line round his fence with names
That we'd never heard of before.

His help in the parish was known
His generosity was deeply shown.

To us East Sutton is known
As John Paine and his farming home.

Natalie Bates (13) Invicta Grammar School

POETRY POEM

I hate to write these poems
They take up all my time,
I find it very hard
To make my lines rhyme.

We write our poems at school
The teacher tells us to,
For competitions and quizzes
Or when we've nothing else to do.

So whilst I write this poem
I'll sit and watch TV
And hope I win a prize
For what this poem should be.

Sara Tozer (15) Invicta Grammar School

A SENSE OF LIFE

A tear of salt
A cry for help
A closed door,
A comfort of warmth
A smile of kindness
A room of light,
A lonely street
A winter's night
A hunger of need,
A cold shadow
A painless day
A never-ending fear,
A nameless person
A silence
A life ends.

Caroline Mills (14) Invicta Grammar School

THE MYSTERIOUS UNIDENTIFIED FLYING OBJECT

Ahh, run it's the UFO again,
Help he'll take us away,
Quick in the house.

The creepy scary sound comes closer to
You as you run faster,
There are children crying.
You can only see the red and blue lights flashing
In your eyes.

If you hide it will surely find you and
Take you away.
It zooms at warp speed in the sky and
Hovers around looking for its next victim.
Watch out, next time it could be you.

James Foster (11) St Edmunds School

THE LITTLE DOG

The little dog,
Has ears long and flappy,
When running in the garden,
She is so happy.
She innocently tramples all the flowers,
Being outside keeps her happy for hours.

Like a propeller,
Her tail waves about,
Her eyes are bright,
Her tongue hangs out.
Almost to the ground her ears hang down,
Her coat is white with patches of brown.

She chases a ball,
And fetches it too,
But chews it and won't give it back to you,
She bounds to the bushes
And disappears from sight,
Oh no! What was that noise?
A gulp and a bite
(I knew we shouldn't have lived next to that rottweiler!)

Mark Taylor (11) Ravens Wood School for Boys

THE WANDERER

Short, fat, orange and hairy,
Prancing around the room like a fairy,
Sitting, lying, eating chocolate,
Sniffing around my master's pocket,
Happy, handsome, with a cold nose,
I like to go where everyone goes,
Night time now, I sleep like a log,
Guarding the house, I'm a very tired dog.

Ian McCamley (12) Ravens Wood School for Boys

GEOFFREY

I'm Geoffrey and I'm a giraffe and a half,
I remember back when I was a calf,
I was top of my class in art and craft,
But once I threw up and boy, did I barf.

It covered the floor, it covered the walls,
It even covered our new sports hall,
I wished, oh I wished that no-one would fall,
Into this sea of sick that frightened us all.

It was a boy from year seven, Horatio Lion,
Who fell in the sick sea when he tripped on
Some iron,
All of his teachers kept trying and trying,
To stop poor Horatio from sinking and dying.

Horatio died, he didn't live anymore,
All the kids in my class were saying Geoffrey
Cor!
That was some sea of sick you threw up in
Room four,
We'd never seen anything like it before.

Adam Reeve (11) St Edmunds School

THE PLOT

Feet running through dark streets
Death in the air
Tempestuous winds through the Doric
Columns
Fire spreading along the streets
Silent whispers
Spirits by bleeding walls
The sound of daggers clashing
The plot is complete.

Richard Lock (13) Northfleet School for Boys

TRAIN TRACKS

You will have your brace in February
The dentist said to me,
I went home all a quiver
And sat down for my tea.

I was not worried how I looked
Just would it cause me pain.
It might just hurt a little bit
But then it would be done.
Then I could get back to life
And have a bit of fun.

Here I am just two days on
And all the pain has gone.
My tracks are here for all to see,
But no more boiled sweets for me.

Robert Bociek (11) St Edmunds School

THE CAT

Out he slinks from his fireplace rug,
Along the alley he makes his way,
Into his own midnight world,
A world that's his alone.

His tail starts swishing from side to side,
Eyes glowing bright yellow,
Fangs shining in the bright moonlight,
Claws at the ready, sharpened the night before.

Back by morning for his early feed,
After being alone in that dark back street.
What does he do? Where does he go?
That is only his to know.

Ross Fullerton (11) Ravens Wood School for Boys

THE TREES

Once long ago there stood some trees,
Tall and graceful, as they blew in the breeze.
They danced and twirled
Their rainbow of leaves
As they stood there enchanted
By the cool, autumn breeze.

Life as we knew it has never been held
In the wooden fingers of the oak and the elm,
They live life as though dead,
No worries and no strife for the oak and his wife.

The trees they do whisper
And have done so for years,
Of man and his lifetimes,
Of his worries and fears.

All of the trees hold the secret of life,
And that is, do not worry, have troubles, or strife.

Rebekah Coughlan (12) Gravesend Girls' Grammar School

THE SNAKE

As it silently slithers through the grass looking
For its prey.
It looks all around ready to pounce on some poor
Creature.
Then he sees it,
He hides behind a bush,
Watching all the time,
Waiting for it to move,
Ready and determined,
His chance comes and he kills the poor thing,
He tucks in and then slithers away.

Harry Bushnell (12) Ravens Wood School for Boys

WHO

Who lives in a sett,
deep underground?
Who's out at night,
makes little sound?
Who searches around
for something to eat?
Who looks in the dustbins
for scraps of meat?

Who is the animal
that comes out at night?
Who is the animal
the hunters want to fright?
Who is the animal
with stripes on its head?
Who is the animal
which is rarely fed?
Who?
A badger!

Christina-Ann Hellyar (12) Holmesdale Community School

A TEDDY BEAR'S THOUGHT

I was bought eight years ago
I was a treasure of treasures
But then I had to go
I had so many pleasures.

I was not pulled or stamped on
Until she wanted a doll
That wasn't very good for me
Because I'm stuck upon the coal.

She probably can't remember me
She used to sit me on her knee
She used to give me a kiss goodnight
And in the morning when it was light.

I went where ever she went
Once we even went to Kent
Sometimes she walked me to a shop
And bought me a bottle of frizzy pop.

I'm gathering dust day by day
She's probably saying hip hip hooray
She thinks I'm just a stuffed old bear
But we do have feelings out there.

Hayley Robinson (11) St Edmunds School

ONE WILD FLOWER

There was one wild flower standing up on its own,
Away from everybody he starts to moan,
In a low deep voice and a sad lonely face
He began to grumble that he was out of his race.

All of his friends died a long time ago,
They all disappeared in one little blow.
A great number of feet started to stamp all around
But he was lucky and ended up safe and sound.

Paul Morgan (11) St Edmunds School

MANCHESTER UNITED

The team in red are the best,
Points and points ahead of the rest,
With players like Giggs including Hughes,
This team of mine will never lose.
Their marvellous skills on the field,
This years championship is signed and sealed,
When Cantona scores,
The crowd just roar,
Along Giggs glides, he just shoots wide.

Lee Thomas (11) St Edmunds School

THE PREYING MANTIS

Just when you thought it was safe,
The Preying Mantis strikes from beneath!
You struggle and strive,
Its grip is too much.
You fight for your life!
You're trapped in its claws,
You can't escape from its jaws!
It's eating you alive,
But it doesn't care.
It thinks it's lucky,
To have a morsel so rare.
Its teeth sink into your flesh,
It's agony but still you're alive to witness the pain,
You are slowly,
But surely,
Falling into a deep,
Deep sleep . . .
And as you lie there,
You are being devoured,
But you do not know this because you are *dead!*

Richard Greene (11) St Johns School

IT'S YOUR DUTY BOY

Trying to overcome the fear,
Is like attempting to walk with two wooden legs.
A death defying nightmare, spinning round and round
In your head like a clock, overcoming time that
Never stops ticking, tick, tock, tick, tock.

The noise is non other than a steamtrain
Chugging, the wheels churning like the pain
Churns in your blood around and around,
The knife that pierced your heart is like
The imprint of a book that is there forever.

Your friend calling out like a vixen calls
Out to her cubs, whining, wriggling in pain,
The cry fades into a distant memory,
One that was wished to be forgotten,
Buried with your friend long gone.

A sharp pain hits your spine, all is forgotten,
You are blind to the world, the clock ticks no more.
The steamtrain screeches to a halt,
All is done, you have done your duty, it's your turn to die
The plain stone memory lives on, and on.

Katy Tapp (13) Weald of Kent Grammar School For Girls

THE WHALE

The whale is the largest
mammal in the sea,
they are as gentle,
as can be.
They breach out of the water
to dive more deeper,
so they can catch fish
for their dinner.

The whaling ships
put out to sea,
harpoons are ready
for a kill,
a flashing tail is spotted
nearby
and the harpoon
is put to flight.
Another whale
is just a memory.

Nicola Peake (12) Holmesdale Community School

THE TELEGRAM

Standing in the mud,
On someone else's land,
Shells illuminate the landscape,
And bullets whistle by.

I want to tear it off,
This uniform that I wear,
Is a pride in your country,
Really enough to die for?

Enticed with rum and brandy,
The shrill whistle fills the air,
Shouts of encouragement echo all around me,
But I cannot move.

Am I such a coward,
Thinking of loved ones at home?
Please do not let them know,
I feel the bayonet enter my body.

My wife will not know,
The way it was at war,
A piece of paper is my epitaph,
The telegram announcing my demise.

Carly Rogers (13) Weald of Kent Grammar School For Girls

HOPELESSNESS

A never ending battle of hatred and fear,
No one who'd cared for her, no one who'd hear,
The cries of pain and anguish she'd bear,
Is anyone out there does anyone care?

Alone in her room, with no-one to share,
Her thought's and her feelings, that she loved no longer there,
A mother, a brother, a father, a sister,
None of which had ever kissed her.

Bruises and scars cover her flesh,
Criss-crossing her body like a mesh,
She has no-one to love, no-one to trust,
She just stays in her room and tries not to cry.

The tears in her eyes,
Grow with hatred and despise,
As her emotions boil over,
She feels her life should be over.

Delphine Hinton (15) Weald of Kent Grammar School for Girls

THE MEAN OLD MAN

The selfish man across the road
Is mean and dirty and very old
When we go past he waves his fists
And says *Go away you lousy kids*
We go and play out with our ball
And kicked it over the mean man's wall.
He comes out shouting *go away*
You'll never see your ball again
Then when we turned to go back
Home, he says *what's yours is*
Mine and what's mine's my own.

Charlotte Dorling (12) St Edmunds School

WAR

War as evil as dark as the night
It brings misery and sadness
In the days and night
Pain and suffering
Comes to all who stand in its way
People who fight to save their country
Most end up in a grave
But those that keep a calm head
Live to fight another day.

Daniel Rolfe (11) St Edmunds School

A DAGGER OF SHADOWS

Streets stalked by shadows
Over blood-stained cobbles
Silence all around.
A dagger clatters by Pompey's statue
Tree to tree fire spreading
Like whispers in an ear.
Darkened tempests rage o'er head
Spirits haunt the ancient pillars
Blood and death are near.
Dreams of conspirators fly by.
A dagger in the night
Shrouded by cloaks
Arms bathed in blood
Blades held high.

John Broom (14) Northfleet School for Boys

DREAM GIRL

You love that girl there,
And you can't help to stare,
She is looking at you,
But you don't have a clue
What to do.

You are sweating your guts out,
You feel very stupid,
You want to shout out,
I love you Michelle Munden.

You go over to her,
You say, *How are you?*
You ask her out,
And you're relieved it's all over.

Paul Kelly (11) St Johns School

CLOUDS

The clouds that float,
Above your head.
A silver-white mountain,
Or sometimes blood red.
Can be orange can be pink.
Sometimes smooth,
Sometimes bluff.

Wispy white threads,
Lke enormous cobwebs.
Soaring above the treetops.
Noiselessly gliding,
The bulk of the cloud.
Moves without whisper,
Noise or sound.

Richard Apps (11) St Johns School

SNAKES

Quickly, rushing through the grass,
Hypnotic eyes they send you to sleep,
Slithering slimy through the dirt,
Smoothly.

Hissing at anything that moves,
Not noticing what's around him,
Except his,
Prey.

Working on how to catch it,
Timing his moves and
Hisses,
Got it, his prey
It's gone.

Alex Sawyer (12) Ravens Wood School for Boys

STARVATION - OF A CHILD

An innocent face,
Living in a desperate place,
A world of creation,
A victim of starvation.

Pale black face,
Perched in a vacant space,
His body so weak,
No intention to speak.

Bulging brown eyes,
Stare up at the skies,
Remembering the time,
He reached so high,
Hoping his spirit would never die.

No food, but pain,
All over again,
An emptiness feeling,
Without a single meaning.

He drifted away,
To a place he could stay,
Through the beaming light,
Away from the fright.

Kizzy Packer (15) Weald of Kent Grammar School for Girls

BOSNIA

Bombing goes on everyday and night,
The place I live in has no light,
Everything dull there is no thrill,
Loneliness is that bitter pill.

Water is extremely rare,
Every drop is used as there's none to spare,
Our family has just enough to drink,
Let alone washing and filling the sink.

Our food supply is scarce and low,
To the centre of town we have to go,
This is where we collect our daily bread,
From getting this loaf lots of people are dead.

You see we have no freedom to roam around,
Guns are shooting at anyone found,
The buildings are wrecked and look a mess,
When will they stop and give it a rest?

Suzanne Hackman (12) Weald of Kent Grammar School for Girls

A BETTER PLACE

There I stood,
Stranded and alone
One solitary figure at the mercy of war.
I looked out onto the plane
A desolate land of confusion and anger
And there I remained
Open and exposed to the evils of the world.

My memory of life before
Faded like mist in the late morning.
Desperation and despair was all I knew.
Guns and sirens
Possessed my dreams
Life was a meaningless void.

As the finger of death beckoned
The prospect seemed not so grey.
Before it was a cloud
That loomed high above.
Now it was a saviour
My path to a better place.

Amanda Drabwell (14) Weald of Kent Grammar School for Girls

DRUMMER BOY

As I lie in my grave,
I feel perhaps that I was naive,
To venture from my mothers arms,
At such a tender age.

The mud it stinks above my head,
You see, I am not really dead.
I was left to die and rot,
Mud and blood is all I've got.

In my pain I see a face,
One which is silky soft like lace,
It is my mother smiling down,
She little knows where I am bound,
I think of the paper she will receive
And I grieve.

Laura Crittenden (14) Weald of Kent Grammar School for Girls

EARLY MORNING FRIENDS

Yellow rippled haze,
Shimmering light on her dappled skin,
Quietly I crept to the fence,
The damp fresh grass,
A breakfast tender and juicy.
A noise, a movement, a scurry in the hedge,
Alert ears twitched,
Lips quivered,
I watched as her white tail swayed in the breeze.
I coughed, she whinnied,
The thud of hooves on the dusty ground,
A velvet whiskered nose,
Nestled in my hand.

Abbi Hurst (15) Weald of Kent Grammar School for Girls

DUST

I am but a tender rose,
Tied with iron to the chair of steel,
Mind in tatters,
Soul in threads,
The knife of eternity digs deep,
Into my heart,
Wandering thoughts,
Down an empty passage,
Thorns tear my soft petals,
With blood red hate.
Rejection tumbles down on me,
Crushes me,
I wither,
My petals crumble to dust.

Katherine Hudson (13) Weald of Kent Grammar School for Girls

STREETS OF LONDON

On the streets of London
People are in the streets
The children come from broken homes
At night you hear the children moan
In the daytime a man asks for a loan
People wish they had of known
Please lend me a penny
For my wife and child
Can't you see
We cannot live out here for much longer
We cannot even afford a bag of crisps.

Here you are it's not much
Thanks ever so much
That's OK we know it's going into good hands.

Gary Wood (11) St Johns School

TWENTIETH CENTURY

I've seen the world you people are wrecking,
It was such a beautiful place,
Smoke is building, people dying, what a
Disgrace!
People robbing, people murdering, this
Isn't a human race.
When will you all realise these are
Great not little mistakes?
If people stop using CFC's and
Other products like that,
The world will be a better place
And not as dark as a bat.
So remember all you earthlings you've only
Got one world.
So try to make it a better place and God in heaven
Proud.

Adam Warren (12) St Johns School

OUR WORLD

The world is dying,
The people are crying,
The ocean birds are no longer flying,
The smoke and fumes are spreading.

Countries are at war,
Countries need money even more,
Countries go against the law,
Countries and people are poor.

People spread chemicals in the sea,
People are affected, just like you and me,
People clean up your dirty deeds,
People of the earth, do not muck up your
World . . .

Kevin Monk (12) St Johns School

THE RAPID WIND

Fire swirling
Rapid winds
Spirits jeering
Evil laughing
People picked up
And dropped
By the devilish wind
Blood curdling
Screams and shouts
Running feet
And always evil
All around.

Steven Bailey (14) Northfleet School for Boys

WAITING

Sitting in the dentist's chair
Feeling mighty sick,
I wish he'd get it over with
Quick, quick, quick.

I can hear tormented screams
Coming through the walls.
What will become of me,
What fate will I befall?

I'm slowly starting to panic,
The adrenaline's begun to pump,
The dentist's fainted, he's on the floor
In a messy lump.

I'm running out of things to say,
The pain, it's getting stronger.
I hope the dentist comes round soon,
I can't bear this pain much longer.

Katherine MacMahon (16) St Mary and St Joseph's School

A PERFECT WORLD

What a miracle it would be,
To see all bad creations great and small,
Shrink down to size at God's beck and call,
All the time we're waiting for,
A new ozone layer and end to war,
A cure to make us live forever more
And help for every child in the street.
We all hope that this will happen,
To see Mother Nature at her best,
Putting everything right what once went wrong
We'll hope and pray
That we might live to see this day,
What a perfect world it would be.

Adrian Lee-Delisle (12) St Edmunds School

HOMEWORK

In you come, slam down your bag
Remember homework, what a drag.
Go upstairs, find a pen,
Settle down to it and then
There's a knock on the door what a bother,
Oh no it's my little brother,
Get rid of him, find that pen
Let's hope he won't be back again
Settle down, it's history
What the teacher wants is a mystery.
Slog for hours, slave away what a pain
It's due next day.
Here we go almost done
And Neighbours has just begun.
Wait a sec, will this do
Or will I be put down to set two.

Andrew Jeffrey (11) The Westlands School

REINVIGORATED

The sun peaks through the leaves,
That belong to the huge trees,
They seem to have no end
And cast immense shadows.
The moist dew drips from their leaves,
Another droplet lands in my arms,
To join the transparent film of water,
That covers my skin.
And the moist, humid atmosphere engulfs me,
It causes my hair to cling to my head.
I am caught up in a world, strange to me,
Yet I feel an unusual sense of calm,
I feel surrounded by this amazing beauty,
The huge green leaves,
They remind me of a fresh summer morning,
The aromas that fill the damp air
They make me feel reinvigorated.
The sounds vibrate every inch of my ear,
Hundreds of different sounds, every animal,
Forms an amazing sound, I feel far . . . far . . .
Away.

Laura MacIntyre (14) Weald of Kent Grammar School for Girls

HEDGEHOGS TRAVEL

I have a love for hedgehogs
which no doubt you can see,
as most of them are dead
with lots and lots of fleas.
When I go to school each
morning and it's not so near
for that,
all I see are hedgehogs
squashed and dead and flat.

Ross Watson (11) St Johns School

THE DOOR

Human by a twisted accident of birth,
Born into the wrong life.
Sliding down to self-destruction,
The zenith of life,
Yet despising it.
Driven to destruction by a longing for the impossible,
Shutting the doors one by one,
Would rather hurt than be hurt,
Turn the key in the lock.
Now happiness, solitude, self abuse,
Shut the door but watch it dissolve,
Looks so easy to leave,
The way out was clear,
But now the path is lined with doubt, regret,
The open door stops the transition,
Reaching to shut it, but can't.
Knowledge of the inevitable,
One day the door will shut.

Libby Fender (16) Weald of Kent Grammar School for Girls

THE SPELL

A witch decided to try out a spell,
To send a prince into hell,
So she sent for a snail
That came with the mail.

She read the spell over and over,
While on holiday in Dover.
Then when she returned home,
The prince would no longer roam.

Then, with a flurry,
She began to hurry.
Word by word,
It was absurd!

Send the prince to his doom
And make his sister prick herself on a loom.
Well, that was how it translated,
The rest is rather complicated.

In the end the spell was wrong,
But it had an effect that lasted long.
And the witch was sent to a castle,
To look after a little rascal.

Kimberly Prebble (13) Weald of Kent Grammar School for Girls

PARADISE

A gentle breeze disturbs the salt water,
A stream slowly trickles its winding way,
Waves of scorching heat ripple the air,
Waves of loneliness drown my despair.

A swaying tree, my everlasting temporary bed, shades me,
Its sweeping branches fan the sand I rest on.
Its sweeping branches sigh with me
As I stare intently at the blurred horizon.

Behind me angry mountains glare at my familiar back,
The curtain like forest veils its life,
But when I move it twitches, draws back,
Eyes appear slowly silently observing.

Then birds swoosh to the air in one enormous rush,
They suddenly disappear, hidden again,
The curtain closes completely, eerie silence returns.
Some floating feathers are the only trace of life.

Except me,
Fixedly gazing out to sea,
Watching, waiting for a boat, another day passes by,
Tears choke my eyes.

Rebecca Laird (14) Weald of Kent Grammar School for Girls

FLY ON THE WALL

A fly on the wall is such a minor being,
But everything around him he is seeing.
Colours and faces,
Decorations and games.
Happiness is very rare.
I love to stare at happy faces,
Happy games and happy places.
But happiness can turn so sour.
Flames of fright, flames of fear,
Arguments can take over power.
But so many memories are dear
And life is too short for a fly.
He sees so much, more than we ever could,
Even before we die.

Lynsey McFerran (15) Weald of Kent Grammar School for Girls

THE WORLD ISN'T A NICE PLACE

The world isn't a nice place
People in the streets make sure they keep their pace.
People try to keep inside, don't want to go out,
For criminals are lurking about.
Stay at home be safe,
Not having any faith,
Naughty boys throwing stones.
Old ladies at home alone.
People dying every day.
People working hard for pay.
In the office day in, day out.
Hoping things work out.
Unemployment rising fast.
Not like it was in the past.
The world can be a nice place but
Stay at home just to be safe.

Stewart Spears (11) St Johns School

THE MOON'S NEW HOME

I look up and see the empty sky
With just a slick black film,
Stars look sad without a ruler
Scattered carelessly around.

My eyes wander to the lake
Beholding many beauties,
Quivering with a ghostly effect
Shimmering silently on water.

The mighty moon now helpless,
Captured by the deep, dark pool,
Struggles and ripples on the surface
Forcing itself against power.

Slivering along satin waves
Sending sparks to the stars,
Glistening among glimmers of light
Wondering for its new found home.

Rebecca James (13) Weald of Kent Grammar School for Girls

AN ABUSED CHILD

I sit there just staring into space
Listening to the noises of the day.
Cars whizzing, people talking, people laughing,
The tears fall down my face
Like drips from a tap, slowly one by one.

The aching feeling inside me never goes,
It hangs there reminding me of the pain,
The agony, the distress,
I feel all alone, nobody cares.
Can't somebody spare some time?
Before it's too late.

Clare Harris (14) Weald of Kent Grammar School for Girls

THE HEADACHE

A transformation,
From dark to light.
The fences blurred,
With dizziness spinning.
Around, around,
Constant pain,
To clutch one's head
In grief, in agony.
Torrential hail,
Hitting the spot,
Buzzing humming,
The draining,
The loss of energy,
Sucked in a hollow,
To the bottom of the pit,
The tension mounts,
The catch is sprung.

Amy Wilkinson (14) Weald of Kent Grammar School for Girls

ALONE

As buses thunder past
And black taxis finish for the night,
I lie in a box cold and rigid,
My hands senseless, my arms motionless.

The nights are long and dormant,
The streets are lifeless and bare,
I would love to communicate with someone
But no one would even care.

As the sun ascends over the soaring buildings
And roads become full,
I set out on the path to nowhere
Waiting for night-time to fall.

Louise Warren (12) Weald of Kent Grammar School for Girls

ILL

I am nearly always ill,
Guzzling down loads of pills.
Having lots of blood tests done,
Enough to fill the garden pond,
It's always happening to me,
That's why I am a bit weak you see.
In and out of hospitals everywhere,
I don't think it's really fair,
I don't mind as such,
But I don't like it very much,
I'd rather be on a horse and play,
And help at the stables all day.
Hopefully one day I'll be well,
Then a different story I will tell.

Yanina Mungar (11) St Edmunds School

THE SEA

On long and sunny summer days,
The tide comes in with gentle waves,
It washes all the golden sand,
And reaches where the sea-gulls land.

But when the winter time is here,
The waves are high and sailors fear,
The sea looks angry, dark and grey,
And smashes on rocks with lots of spray.

Gareth Payne (12) St Edmunds School

IF . . .

If heaven is a place on earth, then show me where it be.
If sadness is a state of mind, then find the paradise in me.
If you are just a little child, then let me find your place.
If beauty lies within the soul then let it show upon my face.

Michelle Small (13) Highworth Grammar School for Girls

THE HAUNTED HOUSE

Creaky floors and squeaky doors,
A winding staircase up the wall.
Although I don't really know this house,
I feel I've seen it before.

Ghosts and ghouls in all the halls,
A creepy voice just called.
Is it my imagination?
Or is this house just old?

As I walk towards the door,
I see something on the floor.
It's black and it's hairy,
Oh it looks so scary.

Chloë Treherne (12) Weald of Kent Grammar School for Girls

ON MY OWN

I sit in the streets, I'm all alone,
The winter is here and I have no home,
A cardboard box is where I live,
The people here are too stubborn to give.

They walk past me without a care,
Whatever happened to my fair share?
Scraps from the street is all I get to eat,
I have rags for clothes and no shoes on my feet.

I beg for money every single day,
But do you think people give to me,
No, no way.
Maybe one day I'll have my own home,
But until that day I'm all alone.

Jemma Richardson (12) Weald of Kent Grammar School for Girls

THE STREET

Walking down the lonely street,
Same old faces that I meet.
Hungry, drunk, gasping for air,
It's not their fault it doesn't
Seem fair.
Someone puts out a dirty hand,
I give him some money at
His command.
I carry on down the lonely lane,
With all the homeless,
It's such a shame.
Is there something we can do?
How would you feel if it were you?
No home to go to, no caring friends,
They rely on money that
Someone lends.
Their faces stare up in despair,
But all they want is love and care.

Stephanie Withycombe (12) Weald of Kent Grammar School for Girls

WAR

Desolate houses, dormant streets,
Lifeless except for the patter of feet,
Of starving children, cold and weak,
Their future seems so empty and bleak,
Helpless cries of pain and suffering,
Of those family's who have nothing,
Still every day is the same,
Don't the guilty ever feel ashamed,
Of the bodies just thrown away,
Like it is just another day.

Sarah Wilson (12) Weald of Kent Grammar School for Girls

SUMMER SUNRISE

The rising sun, above the horizon,
waking the creatures of the night.
Mysterious darkness fading away,
dawn breaking into scattered light.

Colour thrown out onto the world,
every shadow cowering in fear.
Flowers in bloom, with smooth, silk stems
and dried out petals so meek and mere.

Tiny fragments of splintered glass,
firmly place upon the ground,
with only a whistle now and again
and only the wind making a sound.

The summer sun is surprisingly warm,
the touch of the wind is cold on my face.
The spell of the summer is taking its toll
and the cold, chill of winter is taking its place.

Emily Howie (13) Weald of Kent Grammar School for Girls

THE DEADLY SPIDER

The buzzing wings of the fly,
Happily flying through the air,
Suddenly he
Stops!
Only the sound of teeth,
Trying to get through the web,
Of the deadly spider.

The spider pounces without delay,
The fly struggles but not for long,
For the deadly spider's fangs,
Are already half way in.

Simon Williams (11) Ravens Wood School for Boys

HOSTAGE!

Trapped all alone in a world of his own,
the young man in his battered home.
Year after year, he painfully suffers,
all he can manage is lonely mutters.

Kept with the stench of moistness and mould,
his captors, all they do is scold.
All day long, his cries and his weeping,
can be heard while rats are creeping.

Slumped and screwed up in the dirty squalor,
fleas and insects infest his collar.
Cold and wet he can never sleep,
his own possessions, he cannot keep.

Evil spirits live in the men,
who taunt and tease him in his miniature den.
All he wants is to be free,
but all they do is ignore his plea.

Lucy James (14) Weald of Kent Grammar School for Girls

REMEMBRANCE SUNDAY

When Sunday comes and the bugle sounds
A minute's silence falls all around.
An older soldier stands, and he remembers
Each second, an hour,
A year of his life.
Each year is filled with so many thoughts
About him and his friends and the battles they fought.
His heart goes heavy,
A lump comes to his throat,
A voice cries out, *it's over, it's over!*
He begins to cry
And mutters the words, *but why, but why?*

Gareth Hughes (12) St Johns School

SCHOOL TREE

Year seven are the leaves trampled on the ground,
Year eight are the twigs in the wind of life,
Year nine are large branches that cannot break from the tree,
Year ten are the roots feeling blindly through the earth,
Year eleven are the birds nesting in the trees, ready to fly
when they have got what they need.
The teachers are the trunk supporting the rest of the tree,
But trunks can get chopped down,
The headteacher is the gardener in control of the tree,
He can cut down the branches, and sweep away the leaves.

Ross Bone (11) St Johns School

WEATHER

Snowy Siberia
Hot in Australia
The weather doesn't know what to do.

Raining one minute
Sunny the next
Snowing at cold countries
Windy I bet.

Michael Holden (12) St Johns School

CARDBOARD CITY

Cardboard city, screaming cries,
The helpless feeling for those that have died,
Pleading young eyes so cold and alone,
No home to live in, no place to call their own.
A blanket or two to cover their skin,
Warmth to engulf their bodies within,
Looming, black trees to cover their light,
But nothing will cover their tremendous fright.

Philippa Machen (12) Weald of Kent Grammar School for Girls

DRUGS

It's been three weeks now
Since I gave them up
But the craving inside
Will never be up.

I came out in cold sweats
And start to shiver
My mind goes a blank
My hands begin to quiver.

People think they understand
Then they try to help me
But how could they know
When all they do is patronise me.

Will I ever be free
From these devils deep within me?
Or shall I just give up
And let them all beat me.

I can feel my body wrenching
Wanting something to keep it going
My skin is still grey
It has no sign of going.

My parents try to support me
But they think I'm just a thug
Why did I ever get involved
In the awful world of drugs.

Susie Mitson (15) Weald of Kent Grammar School for Girls

THE IMAGE

I walked through the field,
Laughing and talking,
Longing to run, springing and leaping,
The smell of the country captured my breath,
With each new movement, my soul opened,
The wind getting up to challenge the movement.

To touch the fresh leaves, swirling and twirling,
They spin on my fingers like music curling,
I caught sight of my lover, my heart started jumping,
I waved at him, lifting my arms to attract him.
The passion came up inside my mind, I ran down
To meet him, to kiss him and hug him,
When all of a sudden, I realised the obsession
Was all in my head.
There was no-one there, just an image on water.

Philippa Adams (14) Weald of Kent Grammar School for Girls

CONTROVERSY

I might as well be dead,
When will the fighting stop?
I overhear my name,
It is my fault again.

Life is so very strange,
They never comprehend.
Continuously each night,
An unforgivable sight.

More shouting and more tears,
Loud banging and crashing.
As I remain in bed,
I wish that I was dead.

Joanne Napper (14) Weald of Kent Grammar School for Girls

MY CAT

All is still, still as a house,
cat stirs, dreams of a mouse,
paws outstretched like a tiger in wait.
Rabbits coming, soon to be bait.

Claws are sharp, like shining daggers,
smells are strong, must be badgers,
taking off with a thundering leap
gone in search of the biggest treat.

Legs outstretched, leaps are high,
ears are turned, turned to the sky.
Head is turned, tilted to the side
gaily watching birds in glide.

Birds are gone to another hide.
All is still, quite outside.
Turned around to his cosy bed.
Laying down his sleepy head.

Katie Hodder (14) Weald of Kent Grammar School for Girls

SPRING

I see the peaceful view as I pass,
Walking through the succulent grass.
The running stream is crystal blue,
And the sky is turning on orchid hue.

White blossom on cherry trees,
And pollen collected by baby bees.
Little lambs start to fall asleep.
While some choose to leap.

The yellow daffodils start to shine,
Tulips and bluebells stand in a line.
The fresh, floral smell,
As I walk down the silent dell.

Sarah Armitage (13) Weald of Kent Grammar School for Girls

THE DREAM

I sit and stare,
I'm sure it's a glimpse of heaven, but on earth.
A field filled with tall swaying poppies,
As bright and radiant as a baby's beaming face.
Children laughing, their voices melodious.

A stream at the bottom of the field,
Sparkles in the golden sunlight.
A hazy atmosphere,
Delicately fragranced with the sweet smell
Of a summer breeze.

As I dance gracefully along the stream,
My foot slips.
I bang my head on the side of the bank.
Then I open my sore eyes,
Look up to the black sky, it's in pain.

I slowly limp up the dying field,
Drenched with my own tears.
A small child bumps into me on her bike.
Sorry she says.
Don't worry I replied,
It's not your fault.

Jessica Mardel (15) Weald of Kent Grammar School for Girls

MELANCHOLY

Excessive sadness, no hope left,
Inactivity, silence,
Depression seeps into the inner soul,
Stagnation haunts the room,
Despondent at exuberance,
Plundering vigour,
Never ending the breath of depression.

Katie Clayton (14) Weald of Kent Grammar School for Girls

WHY?

I walked rhythmically down the path,
The sound of cars buzzing in my ears.
My eyes stared blankly ahead
Watching but not really noticing - almost as if dead.

The car came around the corner,
I was only vaguely aware of the speed it moved at.
I didn't notice the bike coming the other way,
Perhaps if I had, a life would be saved.

The crunch of the wheels, the crack of the glass,
The screech of the brakes and the cry that she made
All blended to one ear piercing shriek
Before leaving a silence, feelings turned weak.

I look back on that day and my heart fills with pain,
A sense of overwhelming guilt forms a cloak around me,
A cloak of iron - impossible to demolish
And I ask myself -
Why did it have to be me that God chose to punish?

Kirsty MacDonald (14) Weald of Kent Grammar School

RAIN

The clouds in the sky,
Were filled with gloom.
Thicker and greyer they became.
The washing on the lines was collected in haste,
As the first drops of rain began to fall.

The shoppers in town,
Together did frown,
As they fumbled for their umbrellas.
The wind picked up,
The sky turned black
And the rain fell in torrents.

Emma Hollander (15) Weald of Kent Grammar School for Girls

ALONE

Lying there,
All alone,
No-one cares.

Warmth is a wonder,
Caring is a fantasy,
Moving in their minds.

The trees are their shelter,
Cardboard boxes are their friends,
Whispers are their cries.

Wishing for love,
Wishing for strength,
Wishing for death.

Rachel Malpass (12) Weald of Kent Grammar School for Girls

YOUR CHOICE

The screams ring out and echo around,
Before their sudden death,
The burning pits that have no end,
As they gasp their final breath.

The ruler's laughter that haunts the mind,
The faces that show the pain,
The helpless souls now paying the price,
The devil is enjoying his game.

Above the clouds, the world is calm,
The pearly gates invite,
This paradise so tranquil,
The land that shines so bright.

The trees bear fruit that blossom all year,
The harmony of life together,
Utopia, unique in a world of its own,
All hatred lost forever.

Lisa Moore (13) Weald of Kent Grammar School for Girls

SIGHT

I reached out my hand,
His coat was warm and silky.
He helped me to forget,
The darkness of this land.

The cloudiness was clearing,
My protector, my leader,
He is my life, my guide, my friend
And no more was I fearing.

Out of the mist came sight,
The centre of my world,
His lead is my lifeline
And I can live to fight.

Emma Banfield (15) Weald of Kent Grammar School for Girls

ALL ALONE

I stare at the mirror and gaze in despair,
Why oh why is life so unfair?
I think to myself what a terrible sight,
All I can see is a winters night.

Why should it matter, my colour and creed,
Surely that isn't enough to need?
To call me names and give me glares,
To steal my books for funny dares.

Why can't you see what you're doing to me,
Oh how I wish I could run free
From cruel words and glaring faces,
While you laugh and play and run in races.

Life isn't fun when you're on your own,
No-one to talk to , having to sit alone.
But I hope someday you'll understand why,
All I want is to give up and die.

Lisa Howland (15) Weald of Kent Grammar School for Girls

LIVING IN A SILENT WORLD

So many problems on my path,
Thousands of barriers in my way.
Frightened footsteps which I can't hear,
As lonely as a single tear.

When I try to speak, they try not to laugh,
If only they knew how I felt but
People ignore me as though I'm not there,
They hurt me so much as if I don't care.

I'm engulfed in sadness
And wrapped in silence.
No-one knows just how I feel,
But this is something which never heals.

All through the day I constantly turn,
I'm terrified of what's behind me.
I feel so frustrated but what can I do?
As nobody knows the pain I go through.

People are cold, cruel and inhuman,
I feel like I'm sentenced, without a crime.
I desperately want to make them pay,
But maybe they will, be punished one day.

Vanessa Kingwell (14) Weald of Kent Grammar School for Girls

IT'S REAL

They never understand the way that I feel,
I have tried to convince them my feelings are real.
They don't want to know, they just don't believe me,
But God is so real and His spirit within me.

He matters to me, many things don't,
I try to make them understand but they just won't.
I tried to tell them who he is, but they just don't seem to care,
I've told them he is still alive, and he is everywhere.

They just laugh and tease me more,
And as I fall to my knees upon the floor,
I pray out loud that they may welcome his spirit in,
And draw near to him, and repent of their sin.

They laugh at this, so I try to explain
The reason I do this again and again:

You don't understand, you've never believed,
The holy spirit you've never received;
If only you knew, if only you cared,
The things we could have changed; the things we could have shared.

So as I sit and pray, I hope all turns out well,
I hope my friends believe me, I can't let them go to hell.
So please do help, Lord of all that is pure,
Help us to find a miraculous cure.

Kirsty Shillingford (14) Weald of Kent Grammar School for Girls

HOMELESSNESS

Left alone,
Left outside,
Not knowing which way to turn.

Lost in a world of fear
Cold and bare
Wishing for love
Wishing for a home.

A cardboard box
The clothes on their back
Are all their possessions for life.

Love is a wonder,
A home, a fantasy,
A one way street, to sorrow.

Katie Smith (13) Weald of Kent Grammar School for Girls

A FIELD OF FLOWERS

There once was a field of flowers
They were red like fire, yellow like the sun
And white like ghosts.
The wind would blow and the flowers would
Sway like kites in the wind,
I really liked that field of flowers with
Its fire, its sun and its ghost.
But now all the flowers have disappeared
And it is just grass, green like a large
Tired dragon, swaying to music in the wind.

Camilla Fairbrass (12) The Westlands School

DEATH OF MY DAUGHTER

As I walked into the room
And saw her lying there,
Her face was pale and battered blue,
I stroked her wavy hair.

I ran my hand along her face
And felt that life was gone,
The innocent girl that I brought up,
Her love will still live on.

I'll never hear her laugh again,
I'll never feel her touch,
I'll never see her eyes so bright,
I'll miss her, oh so much.

Cathy Manning (12) Weald of Kent Grammar School for Girls

THE DESERT

As I sit on the burning sand,
I can see for miles and miles,
Sand dunes reach up for the sky,
Not a drop of water to be found.

A gust of wind sends sand flying,
Flying in the calm blue skies,
Hot sand blows against my legs,
Scorching my skin, settles in my clothes.

The wind dies down and all is quiet,
I give my leg a shake,
Red hot sand comes flying off it,
As if I'd met my fate.

Leanne Wickenden (13) Weald of Kent Grammar School for Girls

THE WILLOW

I stand beneath your limbs
You wave and sway and cling to me
Through wind and rain, you cling to me,
So sad, upset you seem.

As wind strikes earth
You shelter me
You care, caress and comfort me
One among millions, you rescued me
I belong to you and you to me.

Ann Murray (14) Weald of Kent Grammar School for Girls

THE SEVEN STAGES OF A LION

First a cub as helpless as a mouse in a cat's grip,
Next when weaned waits patiently as a potentate waiting for an
Offering of food,
His eyes as bright as the stars as he played with his siblings,
As he grows older he stalks his fellow cubs as a man might
Stalk his enemy in battle,
The young male has to find new territory and fend for himself
As an orphan might do in a war torn country,
The adult lion Romeo needs to find himself a Juliet,
King of all the beasts surveys his kingly pride.

Kelly Ward (12) The Westlands School

THE UNINSPIRED

Staring into endless space,
I seek words, inspiration,
Clueless, no dream or idea,
Wind whistles through
My mind, drying
Up my imagination,
Like flowers wilting,
Dying in piercing sunlight.
My paper blank,
My mind seeking,
Searching for words to
Express my feelings.

Gayle Stevens (14) Weald of Kent Grammar School for Girls

THE STORM

As the sun was setting low,
A steady breeze began to blow,
Colours and shapes faded away,
Not to come back until the next day.

The first drops of rain fell onto the trees,
As the now strong wind, rustled the leaves,
Thunder boomed out in rage,
As if trapped in an iron cage.

Bright streets of lightening split up the sky,
Like jigsaw pieces up on high
And from the shattered heavens rain did fall,
As I ran to the sight of my front door.

Home at last and out of the storm,
It was comforting to be dry and warm,
The stress and pain of the day,
Seemed to just fade away.

Fantasy filled my empty head,
As I slowly got up and went to bed
And thought about how the birds sing,
Hoping that would be what the next day would bring.

Michelle Maslin (13) Weald of Kent Grammar School for Girls

MY POLKA DOT SOCK

Today
a man came
to service the
washing machine.

He opened the bottom
out came
my polka dot sock.

So
that's where
it went.
The man
got such a shock
when he saw my
polka dot sock.

Samantha Stonham (12) The Westlands School

THE FALL OF DARKNESS

The sun sinks into the earth,
Making the earth roar with life,
Leaving the sky on fire,
The dimness closing in,
The sky now as clear as water,
The moon lighting the sky.
Like a white chocolate button floating around,
The bulb like stars dazzle overhead,
Now it's time to go to bed!

Jeannine Cox (12) Weald of Kent Grammar School for Girls

LONELINESS

Every day my life is the same,
To the bullies it's all just a game,
Making my life hell,
But I don't dare to tell.

They bully me night and day,
All I ever do is pray,
That God will take away the pain,
Of the thugs childish game.

Ignore them and they will go away,
Is what everyone would say,
The teachers or my mum,
It's just a bit of fun.

But they don't know how it feels,
To be their punch bag on wheels,
They punch and kick, thump and fight,
That is what happens day and night.

Sharon Webb (13) Weald of Kent Grammar School for Girls

DEAD

Stale water,
Dripping into darkness.
An endless pit,
With a shape so certain.
An artificial force,
Controlling the mind.
Melted wax,
Hardened by fear.
An endless lifetime,
Never to be lived.

Abigail Beatson (13) Weald of Kent Grammar School for Girls

SNAKE IN THE JUNGLE

A snake slithers slowly through the jungle,
His smooth slippery scales scratch the tall green grass.
He makes a soft subtle rattling sound,
His deadly fangs slip in and out simultaneously
He searches in hope,
Of finding something to eat.
A sleek scavenger,
Scanning every square centimetre of the jungle,
A spider lingers around nearby,
Minding its own business,
Their eyes meet,
The spider stares in horror,
It scuttles away, terrified,
But the spider's speed,
Is no match for the snake,
Gulp!
With one swift move,
the spider is gone,
Dead, eaten, finished,
Still the starving snake,
Continues his desperate joumey,
To satisfy his hunger.

Daniel Murfet (11) Ravens Wood School for Boys

MOONLIGHT DEATH

Wandering drearily across the dusty land,
Not getting anywhere, she's sinking in the sand.
Searching for her long lost cubs,
Looking for the ones she loves,
They wandered off so very young,
One was wounded, had been stung,
Listening for their desperate cries,
In her grief, she nearly dies.
Her throat is dry, her leg is lame,
Hoping this was not a game.
The sun disappears, the stars come out,
In the back of her mind, there is no doubt,
Her cubs have gone, they must be dead,
She knows it in her weary head.
In her mind, she has to go on,
To look for cubs that must have gone.
She needs to sleep, she wants to dream,
Of all the happy times she's seen.
She drops to the ground beneath the moon,
The moonlight death has come too soon.

Hannah Brunskill (12) Weald of Kent Grammar School for Girls

SLEEP

Sleep creep slowly upon me,
Whispering calling to my
Consciousness to rest, to relax.
My eyelids become heavy,
Magnetically attracted.
The air is infected by the
Mellowness of restful sleep,
My mind is drifting steadily,
Drawn towards the gaping chasm of
Sleep.

Helen Oxley (15) Weald of Kent Grammar School for Girls

SAREJEVO 1993

They don't realise what they're
doing yet.
They don't even care. I think
they forget
that the people they kill and
fill with fright,
they used to have a drink with
every night.
To kill and to maim they try
and they try.
When I see them doing so I could
break down and cry.
Thousands hurt, injured and
dead.
The people doing this must be
sick in the head.
Why do they hate and fight
each other?
Don't they realise they are
all brothers?
They don't realise what they're
doing yet,
They don't even care. I think
they forget.

Andrew Sanchez (12) St Johns School

BEYOND IMAGINATIVE TIME

If such time was foreseen
It would be distinctively vague
A time zone beyond human control
A time which nobody could predict events
Only God would know the chronological order
Beyond imaginative time.

A blanket of mystic stars
Watch like an angel over the night
Where dreams so fragile
Fade and disappear
Without leaving a trace
Beyond Imaginative time.

Our unknown destiny lies in the realms of time
The stars by which our life is predicted
The future is being determined
Not by what happened yesterday
But by what is occurring now
A timeless zone beyond imaginative time.

What is our time on earth but a blink in time
Before the master's great hand reaches out
And draws us into eternity
Passing from this existence to another world
Beyond Imaginative time.

I am a force
in matter
a movement
in energy
I am a void
without time.

Richard Hancock (14) Swadelands School

ON HOLIDAY?

It was a worry-hurry, quick-scurry kind of day.
It was a whoopee-doo, toodle-loo not the time to play.
It was a knicker-bocker, getting hotter, really scorching
Holiday.
It was a squish-squash, mish-mash,
Double-jointed, head-bash,
Molly-coddle, widdle-waddle,
All day long.
It was an och-aye-the-noo, need the loo, me too journey.
It was a hullabaloo, hilarious too, worse than the wises of
Emie.
It was a boring-warring, squiggle-giggle, hunger-bunger gnawing
- Esso we stopped.
It was a squish-squash, mish-mash,
Double-jointed, head-bash,
Molly-coddle, widdle-waddle,
How many more miles?
It was a moany-groany, huffy-puffy, really stuffy ride.
Mum said, 'If you don't stop arguing, I'll tan your hide.'
It was an I-us spy-us, no-us pie-us, get-off-my-foot,
I'll stuff you up the chimney and cover you in soot.

We're lurching-searching, slowing-whoa-ing,
Excited,
Ignited!
. . . *Whoopee! We're here.*

Beverley Edwards (13) Highworth Grammar School for Girls

WHY ME?

As dawn emerges over the horizon,
My body tightens with fear and excitement.
It remains in my withered, damaged body,
Causing silent trouble, causing despair.

As I wake fully, my feelings of weakness
remain looming over me like a storm.
My deep wounds remind me that my family wait
patiently but without success.

My home's a trench now,
full of dank, dark memories of the time I
spent with my companions.
The mud laps around my war-bitten legs like
a whirlpool as we try to defend our territory.

My ears burn with the piercing voices of war,
of fighting, of death.
Another scream, another yell as my troops fall
like scattered chess pieces on the corpse
embedded ground
More numbers for the death toll.

The bright whistle echoes in my swollen brain,
as I charge like a rhinoceros, across
'No Man's Land', across death

I can almost taste victory as I near the enemy line,
But I feel a searing pain in my chest,
I look down and see the blood, the key to my
way out of this hated war.

As I collapse weakly, the scenes and noises of war,
dim to nothingness.

Lisa Whitbread (14) Weald of Kent Grammar School For Girls

THE DAY THE QUEEN RAN OUT OF MONEY

Oh what a laugh it was that day,
When Queenie blew her cash away.
It's true, she spent it, every bit,
The Queen is but a money pit.
She cried and wailed all day long,
She sang a very mournful song.
It was a sad day in the palace,
But the Banker bore no malice,
He lent her some, which made her day
And soon the Queen was heard to say,
Thanks a lot, now one must dash,
Outside, to spend this new-found cash.
Market stalls and shops galore,
To spend, spend, spend, and spend some more.
Oh no you won't the Banker said,
You'll save that money up instead.
And so the Queen renounced her sin
And saved up in her money tin.

Take note of this most Royal pun,
For being broke is not much fun!

Rebecca Vale (14) Invicta Grammar School

ISOLATION

Universal movement
yet isolation is felt.
We're bordering on
the bounds of reality.
Join us.
Join us where souls
drift free.
Join us
in the subconscious cabaret.

Adam Barnes (14) Barton Court Grammar School

THE CORAL

Underwater beehive,
its swallowing craters
like the moon's surface.
Sucking things into it
like a vacuum cleaner.
The whirlpools in its sides,
swirling water cascading
into black holes,
the lonely and deserted,
greedy sea-monster.

Ian Banks (13) Dover Grammar School For Boys

THE MOTORBIKE

Her framework was perfect in every way.
I could find no fault in her adoming body,
Caressing her voluptuous frame.
I thought how sinful it would be to ride her,
Long,
And hard.
Straddling her, I revved her up,
Her piston gained momentum,
The sparks flashed.
We rode on together in harmony.
Savouring the feeling of ultimate heaven,
We travelled to Eldorado.

Toni Redgrove (15) Highsted Grammar School

ELEPHANTS LOCKED AWAY

We put you in zoos and lock you away,
No more fun just sitting all day.

You're walking around, nothing to do,
While we just stand and stare at you.
Looking through bars, touching your skin,
Do you really enjoy this sort of thing?

Looking so lonely your sad little eyes,
Black and beady, no wild sunrise.
Looking straight forward, then to the side,
No where to go, no where to hide.

People staring, poking fun,
Knowing that you can't harm them.
Feeding you buns then running away,
Thinking that you might scare them.

Now the zoo is closing,
People walk away,
Dropping litter on the ground,
Walking to cars and driving away.

It's just another day to them,
They'll go home and eat their tea.
While you're just thinking standing there,
Thinking of forests and being free.

Jennifer Grogan (13) Holmesdale Community School

WHY ME?

I often look in the mirror and think, why me?
The reflection just stares back.
It has no answers,
It just provides a past.
Something to shout at,
Something to be honest with.
But, if you look beyond the face,
What can you see?
Perhaps you'll find an answer,
Perhaps you'll solve the problem.
But, I often find a confused person, whispering,
Why me?

Elisabeth Madden (15)
Weald of Kent Grammar School for Girls

ELEPHANTS IN DANGER

How could they do it: shut you away?
Where's your mother? Couldn't she stay?
Is she in heaven? Or is she on earth?
Or was she taken after your birth?

Have you got any family left?
Were they killed for their tusks? Or taken by theft?

You look so lonely standing in there,
Nothing to do, no-one that cares,
Can I take you to your proper home?
Where you belong, so you're free to roam.

Your skin is so tough, wrinkly and grey,
Your eyes are staring so far away,
Your flapping ears and eyelids a flutter,
You might be gone soon but it won't matter,
They'll have all they want, ivory and all,
But no more elephants, none at all.

Helen Chapman (13) Holmesdale Community School